Ultimate
John Deere

The History of the
Big Green Machines

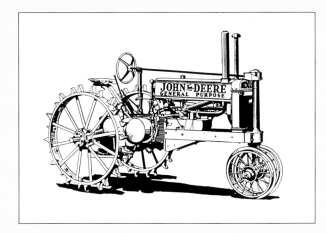

Ralph W. Sanders

Voyageur Press

A TOWN SQUARE BOOK

Edited by Todd R. Berger
Designed by Maria Friedrich
Jacket designed by Andrea Rud
Printed in Hong Kong

01   02   03   04   05   5   4   3   2   1

Library of Congress Cataloging-in-Publication Data

Sanders, Ralph W., 1933-
    Ultimate John Deere : the history of the big green machines / Ralph W. Sanders.
        p. cm. -- (Town Square books)
    Includes bibliographical references and index.
    ISBN 0-89658-406-2
    1. John Deere tractors--History. I. Title. II. Series.

TL233.6.J64 S25 2001
629.225'2--dc21

                                                                            00-043799

Distributed in Canada by Raincoast Books, 9050 Shaughnessy Street, Vancouver, B.C. V6P 6E5

Published by Voyageur Press, Inc.
123 North Second Street, P.O. Box 338, Stillwater, MN 55082 U.S.A.
651-430-2210, fax 651-430-2211
books@voyageurpress.com
www.voyageurpress.com

Educators, fundraisers, premium and gift buyers, publicists, and marketing managers: Looking for creative products and new sales ideas? Voyageur Press books are available at special discounts when purchased in quantities, and special editions can be created to your specifications. For details contact the marketing department at 800-888-9653.

On the frontispiece:
Top: *"Low" and "high" radiator, unstyled Model Gs.*
Bottom left: *The John Deere logo on a 1960 830 diesel.*
Bottom right: *A magazine ad for the ten versions of the Model 420, introduced in 1955.*

On the title page:
Main image: *The 1939 Model H.*
Title inset: *The 1934 Model A, as it appeared in an ad for the brand-new tractor that year.*

Acknowledgments: *A 1938 brochure touting Models A, B, and G.*

Table of contents: *A 1928 Model GP owned by Don and Marty Huber of Moline, Illinois.*

Facing page: *A 1960 4010 diesel tractor owned by farmer-collector Ken Smith of Marion, Ohio.*

Dedication

To Joanne and my children Julie, Scott, David, Richard, Kevin, Neil, and JoEllen. These wonderful individuals give life its true meaning . . . they are its real rewards . . . the priceless returns on life's best "investment."

Acknowledgments

Most of the photographs in this book I created for use in calendars from two publishers. Calendar Promotions, Inc., of Washington, Iowa, has published its *Classic Farm Tractors* calendar each year since 1990, in a venture originated by John Harvey Communications of Wilmington, Delaware, as a promotional piece for DuPont Agricultural Products' *Classic* soybean herbicide. *Historic Farm Tractors* and *Classic John Deere Tractors* are calendars pub-

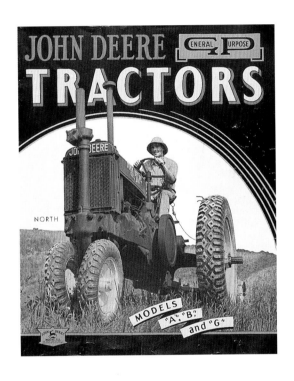

lished annually by Voyageur Press, Inc., of Stillwater, Minnesota, this book's publisher. I want to thank John Harvey of John Harvey Communications, Jim Ratcliff of Calendar Promotions, and Michael Dregni of Voyageur Press, for their contributions in making this book possible by initiating the calendar photography.

The Deere & Company archives in Moline, Illinois, was an invaluable source of information and illustrations for the book. I thank archivist Dr. Leslie Stegh and his staff for their time and effort in helping me locate the needed parts to tell the Deere story.

Deere & Company advertising and product brochures are from several sources, including collectors John W. Chenoweth of Urbandale, Iowa, and Don Rimathe of Huxley, Iowa. Other advertisements were the product of hours and hours of digging through piles of musty farm magazines in antique emporiums.

The real heroes of this effort are the tractor collectors and restorers who have revitalized the wonderful old machines with the thousands of hours and dollars they have invested in finding the tractors, acquiring them, and then bringing them back as "new" machines for us to enjoy as an important chapter of American agriculture's history. The tractor owners who gave me the opportunity to preserve their tractors on film broadened their contribution to the history of the machines that we share with you on these pages. For all of their enthusiastic cooperation, time, and patience, I want to thank the John Deere tractor owners whose machines I have photographed during the past eleven years. They include: Bruce Aldo, Westfield, Massachusetts; Ford Baldwin, Lonoke, Arkansas; Wayne and Cindy Beckom, Kokomo, Indiana; Doug Bockey, Spencerville, Ohio; Dick Bockwoldt, Dixon, Iowa; Wayne Bourgeois, Kahoka, Missouri; George Braaksma, Sibley, Iowa; Edwin Brenner, Kensington, Ohio; Leonard Bruner, Rising City, Nebraska; Bill and Suzanne Burch, Sikeston, Missouri; Ken and Bob Burden, New London, Iowa; Ron Coy, New Richland, Minnesota; Randy Griffin, Letts, Iowa; Bruce Halverson, Huxley, Iowa; Verlan Heberer, Belleville, Illinois; Ed Hermiller, Cloverdale, Ohio; Bob and Mark Hild, Webster City, Iowa; Gerald Holmes, Janesville, Minnesota; Don and Marty Huber, Moline, Illinois; Mel Humphreys, Trenton, Missouri; Tommy and Doris Jarrell, Wilmington, Delaware; Ron Jungmeyer, Russellville, Missouri; Richard Kimball, West Liberty, Ohio; Tom Manning, Dallas Center, Iowa; Don McKinley and Marvin Huber, Quincy, Illinois; the late Ken Peterman and his son Dan Peterman, Webster City, Iowa; James Proctor, West Chester, Pennsylvania; Don Rimathe, Huxley, Iowa; the late Donald Rogers, Atlanta, Illinois; Chad Reeter, Trenton, Missouri; the late Bill Ruffner, Bellevue, Nebraska; Jim Russell, Oblong, Illinois; Lewis and Steve Schleter, Princeton, Indiana; Earl Scott, Marysville, Ohio; Lloyd Simpson, Monroe, North Carolina; Ken Smith, Marion, Ohio; James and Terry Thompson, Laurelville, Ohio; Jeff Underwood, Dahlonega, Georgia; Robert Waits, Rushville, Indiana; David Walker, Chillicothe, Missouri; Don Ward, Chula, Missouri; Mike and Jackie Williams, Clinton, Iowa; Bruce Wilhelm, Avondale, Pennsylvania; and Bill Zegers, Newton, Iowa.

I very much appreciate the patient cooperation and help that you all gave me in making the photographs. John Deere collectors individually, and as a group, are veritable founts of knowledge about the machines they collect. They all shared that information with me unstintingly. Thank you very much, one and all!

Black-and-white line drawings of some draft animals that impacted agriculture and some early John Deere advertisements are from Paul C. Johnson's books *Farm Animals in the Making of America, Farm Power in the Making of America,* and *Farm Inventions in the Making of America,* last published by the Institute for Agricultural Biodiversity (IAB) in Decorah, Iowa. The institute operates a conservation program for endangered farm animal breeds and shows some of them at its Farm Park at 730 College Drive, Decorah, Iowa 52101.

The late Paul C. Johnson, was a longtime editor of *Prairie Farmer* magazine, the venerable farm publication with continuous publishing roots dating back to 1841 in Chicago. It was my good fortune to have Paul as an editor and mentor during my stint as Illinois field editor for the magazine from 1964 until 1968. I continue to appreciate the guidance and feel for Midwestern agriculture he, and my service with the magazine, gave me.

Copyreading help came from Don Huber, a veteran Deere & Company copyeditor and avid John Deere tractor collector; John W. Chenoweth, an engineer and another loyal John Deere collector; and Todd Berger at Voyageur Press. Michael Dregni at Voyageur Press has guided me through two earlier books and has always kept me from taking too many sidetracks. So too did Todd on this project.

My sincere thanks to all of you for your help in making this book possible, for making it interesting, and, I hope, meaningful as well.

Ralph W. Sanders

Contents

John Deere Develops with the Corn Belt

T he history of Yankee blacksmith John Deere and the farm implements his company developed parallels the settlement and harnessing of the native prairies of the Midwest into a veritable food basket now known as the Corn Belt. The prairie came first, of course, its vast "seas" of grass developing from physical conditions and sediments provided by the several ice advances and retreats of the Pleistocene geologic epoch. The first white settlers arrived on the prairie in the 1830s and, not long after, began to till the fertile soil. By the 1870s, once the vast grasslands were settled, plowed, and planted, Deere's company was hard at work making and selling an ever widening variety of tillage tools. Many of Deere's implements were developed to help cultivate maize, or corn, a native grain of the Americas that played a major role in the settlement and development of the United States.

Above: *A farmer works a cornfield on a John Deere Model A.*

Opposite Page: *Corn Belt harvest sunset.*

Tall prairie grasses once stood as high as a horse.

Early settlers kept mostly to the woods. Their fields tended to "emerge" from the forest as trees were cut for buildings, fuel, and fence rails. This scene is at the Lincoln Boyhood National Memorial near Gentryville, Indiana, the site of Abraham Lincoln's family farm from 1816 to 1830.

THE FERTILE INTERIOR

At the beginning of the 1800s, very little was known about the agricultural promise of the Midwestern interior, even after the Lewis and Clark expedition up the Missouri River in search of a water route to the Pacific in 1804–1806. Indeed, for years after the expedition, settlers kept close to the wooded stream valleys. Farmers preferred to establish homesteads along the streams where woodland provided plentiful building material, fuel, and fencing in the form of rails that could be split out of the hardwood logs.

But by the 1820s, wide-ranging honey collectors, trappers, and other peripatetics and adventurers began to leave the river valleys and venture "inland" in search of bee trees, furs, and land routes west. Such observers brought back stories of a seemingly boundless land.

By the 1830s, some settlements bordered the edge of the timber, and venturesome farmers tried their hand at cropping the open prairie—land they wouldn't have to clear.

At first the prairie settlers favored hard winter wheat as their main crop, as this wheat had a known market: Hard winter wheat, which mills out to a better bread flour than soft winter wheat, was needed by millers to grind into flour for bread. The prairie farmers also planted barley, rye, oats, and hay, to provide both food for their family and feed for their livestock. Soon they added corn to their crops to supplement the small grains with which they were most familiar.

MORE PRECIOUS THAN SILVER

Indian corn, a type of flinty maize similar to today's popcorn, had been a life saver in the 1620s for the Pilgrim settlers in what became New England: Stores of corn from Native Americans kept the Pilgrims from starving during their first winters in the New World. The grain was also highly prized in other more southerly early settlements. In 1624, Plymouth Plantation Governor William Bradford wrote of the attitude his settlers developed toward the grain after five years in North America, "They began now highly to prize corn as more precious than silver, and those that had some to spare began to trade one with another for small things, by the quart, pottle [half gallon], and peck etc; for money they had none, and if any had, corn was preferred before it."

As the early settlers, their descendants, and later colonists developed their agricultural practices in the seventeenth century, Indian corn became increasingly accepted as a farm crop, both for food and feed. A growing number of family recipes utilized the grain, ranging from johnnycake and corndodger to hominy and grits. Their livestock, they soon learned, could also prosper from the new crop. Pigs and steers could fatten on corn; cows and oxen could sustain themselves on the fodder from the stalks. Cattle and hogs fattened on corn and cornstalks in central Illinois were driven overland in droves of 750–1,000 head for 100 miles (160 km) or more to packers in Chicago. Farther south in the state, farmers drove their livestock to markets in St. Louis. By the 1870s, the feeding of cattle and hogs became almost totally dependent on corn.

For the early farmers, corn had advantages over wheat, according to historian Allan G. Bogue, in his book, *From Prairie to Corn Belt.* Wheat was subject to insects, disease, and winterkill; it had to be harvested quickly and laboriously for the best quality; and it might yield only twenty to thirty bushels per acre (282–422 l/ha). Corn could yield from forty to sixty bushels per acre (564–844 l/ha) and could withstand a more leisurely harvest stretching through October and November—and sometimes even overwinter into April.

Once the railroads crisscrossed the prairies beginning in the 1850s, corn could roll easily from the farmer to market, and the crop soon outpaced wheat to become the prime grain over the vast, newly settled prairie. At intervals of about every five miles (8 km) along the new railroad tracks, grain elevators sprang up to offer farmers a convenient market just a wagon haul away.

"Corn," stated Chicago-published *Prairie Farmer* in 1864, "supports the poor man's family, the rich man's flask and the merchant's trade. It is the basis of an immense trade in beef, the main pillar of our national prosperity, the golden fleece of America, the staple of the West, the pride of Illinois." And so it was in other states of the prairies.

From about 1870 on, with growing specialization in corn production on the prairies, those lands where corn became the staple crop began to be increasingly called the "Corn Belt," according to Bogue. Today the Corn Belt has as its heart most of Illinois, Indiana, and Iowa, with overflow into parts of Kansas, Nebraska, the Dakotas, Minnesota, Wisconsin, Michigan, Ohio, Kentucky, and Missouri.

RIDING BEATS WALKING

Agricultural industries grew up along with the Corn Belt. As John Deere's plow works in centrally located Moline, Illinois, prospered with the settlement of the prairie from 1848 on, so too did the new Midwestern factories of threshing-machine king Jerome Increase Case of Racine,

Rail corn cribs stored the pioneer's crop as ear corn, for year-long feeding to livestock. This replica is at the working pioneer farm at the Lincoln Boyhood National Memorial.

Wisconsin, and reaper inventor Cyrus H. McCormick in Chicago. Prairie farming and its promise put all three of them in business in the heart of the new country. The prairie's development into the Corn Belt sustained their growth and began to shape their product lines, as products such as grain drills, corn planters, and riding (sulky) cultivators were introduced.

Other tasks were late to be fully mechanized, including corn harvesting, which was only slightly mechanized until the era of the tractor. Horse-drawn corn binders helped farmers cut and bind whole stalks for stacking in shocks. But farmers who grew the crop for its grain, for either animal feed or to sell, were forced to shuck the corn by hand one ear at a time, whether from the shock or from the corn row. Deere became a supplier of corn shellers to remove the kernels from the cob. Early shellers were hand cranked and could shell but an ear or so at a time. Belt-driven steel cylinder shellers, first powered by steam engines and later by tractors, were more productive in doing the corn shelling job.

Power was the key to mechanizing the farms in the

High-stepping draft horses pulling improved lighter-draft farm machines boosted farm productivity as the Corn Belt emerged from the prairies. This seven-horse hitch is pulling a sulky gang plow turning under corn stalks on an Amish farm in Illinois in the mid-1960s.

Corn Belt. At first it was oxen that did the heavy pulling, but the need for speedier power for the improved easier-to-pull farm equipment being made by the new prairie plow factories was increasingly met by horses after the Civil War. And even the original "horse power" was increased in the late 1800s with imported European heavy draft horse breeds providing the stronger pull for the growing need for more farm power.

Deere's company shied away from making steam engines and then the big gas tractors of the early 1900s. Too risky, the board had decided. The company later tried, and canceled, several of its own tractor designs in the early years of the last century before finally deciding in 1918 to buy an established firm and its "lightweight" tractor—the Waterloo Boy. For $2.35 million Deere & Company had a tractor and a tractor factory and was well on its way to finally providing the power units that would help revolutionize farm production. The company decision proved sound. It soon became one of the leading suppliers of

practical farm tractors across the Corn Belt—and across the nation.

GREEN COLLECTORS EVERYWHERE

Through the more than 164 years John Deere farm equipment and tractors have been built, the sturdy, simple, and productive green machines—and the people who made them, sold them, and maintained them—have made hundreds of thousands of friends and fans all over the world. Perhaps that helps to explain the expanding hobby of collecting, restoring, and cherishing the green machines.

The attraction of John Deere two-cylinder tractors as collectible items is a phenomenon of the past thirty-five to forty years that continues to grow to include more recent models. Even the now forty-year-old four- and six-cylinder John Deere New Generation series are already appearing in collections. Wherever you travel in the United States and Canada, there are Two Cylinder Clubs whose activities revolve around finding, collecting, and restor-

Summer parades in rural towns increasingly feature farm tractors of yesterday restored by proud collectors to factory-fresh condition. This "Johnny Popper" parade contingent was photographed at the Western Iowa Antique Tractor Festival at Westside, Iowa, in 1991.

ing Deere tractors. And, those collectors aren't confined to rural areas alone. Even Hollywood, California, and many other metropolitan areas from east to west and north to south have their own John Deere devotees and clubs.

This book outlines the humble start of Deere & Company, its growth into a major supplier of farm equipment in the world, and shows some of the marvelous machines it manufactured to provide the power that revolutionized farming and helped transform the vast prairies into the Corn Belt. The following chapters picture many John Deere tractor models as currently collected and lovingly restored to pristine condition by their fans. It is a delight to share them with you. I hope they furnish you some of the same enjoyment and keen appreciation I have experienced in photographing, researching, and writing about them.

This restored, better-than-new 1936 Model B on steel wheels with hand-lift cultivator sparkles with the meticulous attention collectors Don McKinley and Marvin Huber of Quincy, Illinois, bestowed on this proud tractor in its up-from-rust reincarnation.

Corn became America's "golden fleece" in the 1860s.

Timeline

10,000 BC: Final glacial epoch covering North America receded and prairie soil began to develop from glacial till topped with wind-blown loess.

7000 BC: Primitive strains of maize developed in South America. Native Americans in south-central Mexico began planting early corn varieties beside their squash and beans.

3000 BC: Native Americans in today's southwestern states learned to grow corn.

750–1200 AD: Largest North American city of up to 50,000 Native Americans developed six miles (9.5 km) northeast of today's St. Louis, Missouri, around the area now known as Cahokia Mounds. Ten other Native American towns surrounded the town with another fifty farming villages sprouted nearby. Maize growing was central to the native economy, and trade from Cahokia extended down the Mississippi River to the Gulf of Mexico and upriver into Wisconsin. Cahokia Mounds National Historic Site now marks the ancient city site.

1607: First British colony was established at Jamestown, Virginia. The settlers grew tobacco starting in 1612.

1620: Plymouth Plantation was settled by Pilgrims at Plymouth, Massachusetts.

1621: A member of the Patuxet tribe, Squanto, or more formally Tisquantum, showed the Pilgrims how to plant corn.

The first American Thanksgiving dinner in fall 1621 included food items made from "Indian" corn.

1682: French explorer Robert Cavelier, sieur de La Salle, traveled down the Mississippi River to the Gulf of Mexico and claimed all of the land drained by the big river for France. They named the vast tract Louisiana.

1769: Scottish inventor James Watt patented the steam engine. It was first used to pump water from coal mines and was later modified to power rotary machines using a crankshaft. Steam engines powered the first industrial revolution.

1786: John Fitch tested the first working U.S. steamboat on eastern rivers.

1800s: Soybeans, a legume thought to have originated in eastern China, were introduced into the United States as a forage crop.

1803: The Louisiana Purchase treaty with France signed by President Thomas Jefferson added a huge tract of western land to the United States, including portions of territories that would later encompass the Corn Belt.

1804: John Deere was born February 7 in Rutland, Vermont, the third son of Welsh tailor William Rinold Deere and Sarah (Yates) Deere.

1804–1806: Meriwether Lewis and William Clark explored the new Louisiana Territory and beyond, venturing all the way to the Pacific Ocean via the Missouri River.

1807: Robert Fulton traveled on his steamboat, *Clermont*, 150 miles (240 km) up the Hudson River from New York City to Albany, New York, and opened that river to steam transportation.

1808: The village of St. Louis, Missouri, was incorporated.

1811: The first steamboat traffic appeared on western rivers when Fulton's *New Orleans* traveled 2,000 miles (3,200 km) from Pittsburgh, Pennsylvania, down the Ohio and Mississippi Rivers to reach New Orleans. Seven years later, thirty-one steamboats were running on rivers between Louisville, Kentucky, and New Orleans. St. Louis was served by a growing number of boats, and, by 1840, more than 1,700 boats docked at the city each year as it became a center of shipping on the Mississippi, Missouri, Illinois, and Ohio Rivers.

1825: The Erie Canal opened making water transportation possible from the Hudson River in New York City to Buffalo, and, from there, through the Great Lakes to the Midwest.

1830: The Baltimore & Ohio Railroad started its first railroad in the East. By 1850, railroads had connected most of the eastern United States to the Midwest by rail.

1831: Cyrus Hall McCormick demonstrated a practical grain reaper near Steele's Tavern in Virginia's Shenandoah Valley. He patented his machine in 1834.

1836: Blacksmith John Deere traveled from Vermont to Grand Detour, Illinois, by way of the Erie Canal, Lake Erie, and Lake Michigan. He was looking for opportunities in the new West.

1837: The city of Chicago was incorporated with only 4,853 residents.

1837: The new Grand Detour, Illinois, blacksmith, John Deere, demonstrated a diamond-shaped steel plow made from a saw blade. The self-scouring plow showed promise of turning over the sticky prairie soil without gumming up the plow.

1841: *Prairie Farmer* magazine, aimed to inform the new farmers of the prairie, was founded in Chicago by John S. Wright.

1842: Jerome Increase Case tested and perfected his threshing machine in Racine, Wisconsin. Case's thresher combined elements from a "groundhog" thresher with those of a fanning mill. Case began producing his threshing machine for the market in 1844.

1847: Cyrus McCormick bought the site for his reaper factory on the Chicago River just west of Lake Michigan in Chicago. Reaper production started there in 1848 with 500 machines completed.

1848: John Deere moved production of his self-scouring plow from tiny Grand Detour, Illinois, on the Rock River, to a new site on the Mississippi River at Moline, Illinois. Plow production in the new factory started almost immediately. By 1852, John Deere plow production was reported at 4,000 units annually.

1850s: More efficient steam engines, based on 1849 patents granted to George Henry Corliss, began to power an increasing share of U.S. industry, freeing them from the restriction of locating only near available water power.

1859: Crude oil deposits were discovered in northwest Pennsylvania on Oil Creek near Titusville. "Colonel" Edwin L. Drake's shallow well of about 70 feet (21 m) in depth was the first commercially successful oil well in the United States. Early uses of the new petroleum included the refining of "coal oil," or kerosene, as a lamp and lantern fuel. Gasoline refining soon followed.

1861–1865: The American Civil War divided the United States in a bloody conflict. Southern agriculture and industry were devastated, while northern industry and agriculture were spurred toward higher production levels through greater use of mechanization. Horses and mules began to replace oxen as the farmer's prime power source.

1863: John Deere built the Hawkeye Sulky cultivator, Deere's first implement with a seat for the operator. The cultivator increased the acres of corn that a grower could cultivate.

1868: On August 15, 1868, Deere & Company was incorporated, with John Deere as president and his son, Charles Deere, as vice president. That year the company sold more than 41,000 implements.

1869: The transcontinental railroad was completed when crews building lines from the East for Union Pacific and crews building from the West for Central Pacific meet at Promontory Point, Utah.

1870: Corn had become the dominant crop in the central Midwest, and the Prairie States became known as the Corn Belt.

1875: The John Deere Gilpin Sulky Plow, featuring a seat for the operator, was introduced. The Gilpin design was sub-

sequently improved.

1876: German shop clerk Nikolaus August Otto received a patent on his four-stroke internal-combustion engine. Otto's four-stroke concept was widely accepted, and when his patent expired in 1890, many new gas engines were made using his four-stroke design.

1877: Charles Deere and Alvah Mansur incorporated as Deere & Mansur Company, independent of Deere & Company, to build corn planters. Their Deere Rotary Drop planter was planting corn in 1879 and became a popular planter that joined the Deere & Company product line in 1909.

1885: Karl-Friedrich Benz of Germany built the world's first successful gasoline-driven automobile, a single-cylinder three wheeler.

1880s: Steam traction engines were increasingly used on farms not only to power belt-driven machines but to till the soil with gang plows.

1886: John Deere died on May 17 at the age of eighty-two, nearly fifty years after he began his plow company at Grand Detour, Illinois.

1892: Brothers Charles and Frank Duryea built the first American gasoline-powered automobile, which they drove around on the streets of Springfield, Massachusetts. They soon formed the Duryea Motor Wagon Company.

1892: Custom thresherman John Froelich of Iowa assembled a "traction engine" using a one-cylinder Van Duzen gasoline engine. Froelich's machine was the world's first practical tractor and the "Great" of later John Deere tractors. Froelich saw it as a replacement for heavy steam engines. The company he began, the Waterloo Gasoline Traction Engine Company, soon became the Waterloo Gas Engine Company when the company's focus turned toward stationary engines.

1893: Henry Ford built a car while working as a mechanical engineer with the Edison Illumination Company of Detroit, Michigan. By 1903, he had started the Ford Motor Company, and, in 1908, the first Model T was built. By 1927, Ford had produced 15 million cars.

1895: Rudolf Diesel of Germany invented the diesel engine, which worked on the principle of auto-ignition of a fuel-and-air mixture upon compression.

1902: Hart-Parr in Charles City, Iowa, built its first gas traction engine and later coined the word "tractor" for gasoline traction engines.

1912: Deere & Company authorized the development of a gasoline-powered tractor plow, though work on the John Deere tractor plow stopped in 1914.

1914: World War I started in Europe. By 1917, the United States was involved.

1917: Henry Ford's lightweight tractor, the Fordson, was built in Detroit, Michigan. The mass-produced machine was inexpensive and very popular, and U.S. Fordson sales took off early.

1918: Deere & Company bought the Waterloo Gas Engine Company of Waterloo, Iowa. The two-cylinder 12/25-hp Waterloo Boy tractor became the "Grandpoppa" of all of the John Deere tractors that followed.

1919: John Deere's first tractor design, the three-wheel All-Wheel-Drive, designed by Deere's Joseph Dain, Sr., was produced in Moline. One hundred All-Wheel-Drive tractors were shipped and sold in 1919, but the design was abandoned as being too costly to compete with other tractors, including Deere's own Waterloo Boy.

1923: John Deere announced its all-new Model D. It was a 22/30-hp two-cylinder standard-tread tractor based roughly on the Waterloo Boy but completely reworked with an integral frame and an enclosed final drive. The D was produced continuously from 1924 until 1953 and is considered the "Poppa" of the long line of "Johnny Poppers."

1924: Soybeans were successfully harvested with a combine in central Illinois. That combine demonstration by Massey-Harris Company encouraged the use of combined harvesters east of the Mississippi River. Processed into soybean oil meal and soy oil, the crop soon joined corn as a major crop of the Corn Belt.

1924: A new row-crop, tricycle-configured Farmall tractor was introduced by International Harvester Company of Chicago. It cultivated two to four rows, plowed, disked, planted, and ran PTO as well as belt-driven equipment. The Farmall's success challenged other tractor makers to build row-crop machines.

1926: Hybrid seed corn became available to corn growers, dramatically boosting the corn yields of farmers who tried the hybrids. Corn production zoomed when hybrids were widely accepted in the 1940s. Improved soybean varieties were on the horizon.

1928: The John Deere General Purpose, or GP, tractor was introduced as a three-row, all-crop tractor. A year later, a two-row tricycle GPWT, or wide tread, version was available from John Deere. After a sputtering start, John Deere had planted itself solidly in the tractor business.

1929: The stock market crash of October presaged the Great Depression that devastated American agriculture and industry deep into the 1930s.

1931: Caterpillar built the first diesel farm tractor, the Diesel 65.

1932: Pneumatic rubber tires were factory supplied on farm tractors by Allis-Chalmers.

1934–1935: John Deere introduced the Models A and B tractors, the first Deere tractors to roll on pneumatic tires. The A and B proved to be Deere's all-time best-selling tractors and remained in the John Deere line until 1952.

1937: Deere & Company had some unexpected company when it celebrated the centennial of the John Deere steel plow. Also marking that milestone was the J. I. Case Company of Racine, Wisconsin, which had purchased the Grand Detour Plow Company in 1919, a company started by original Deere partner in plow making Leonard Andrus.

1937: John Deere introduced two new tractors on opposite ends of the power spectrum, the three-plow Model G for larger farms and the one-plow Model 62, which was later renamed the Model L.

1938: John Deere Models A and B got a styling facelift from industrial designer Henry Dreyfuss of New York. The streamlining gave them a solid new modern look.

1939: Looking to smaller-tractor needs, John Deere introduced its one-plow Model H in 1939. It was expected to replace the last team of horses on the farm. The H arrived with styled sheet metal in a two-row tricycle design.

1939: Henry Ford returned to the farm tractor business with the introduction of a revolutionary, lightweight, two-plow tractor, the Ford-Ferguson Model 9N. Its built-in hydraulic control of integrally three-point-mounted equipment was to blaze a trail for modern tractor systems.

1939–1945: World War II raged in Europe and the Pacific Ocean. The United States joined the fray after the Japanese bombed Pearl Harbor in Hawaii on December 7, 1941. John Deere introduced only the GM and LA models during the war period. The new GM of 1941 was a styled G with a six-speed transmission. The LA was a more powerful L.

1940s: Soybean production expanded rapidly in the Corn Belt. First seeded as a drilled crop after small grains in a three-year rotation, soybeans became a row crop in the Corn Belt by the end of World War II.

1945: Deere & Company bought Lindeman Manufacturing of Yakima, Washington, for its crawler track designs. Lindeman had equipped the Model BO chassis with the track units from 1940 to 1947 as the John Deere BO-Lindeman.

1945: The end of World War II saw Deere & Company and other farm equipment makers hustling to meet the pent-up demand for farm tractors. That year Deere bought a factory site on the Mississippi River at Dubuque, Iowa, to give it more tractor-making capacity.

1947: The new John Deere Model M utility tractor with Touch-O-Matic hydraulic implement control was built at the new Dubuque plant. The M was designed to compete with the popular Ford 8N tractor and other new utility tractor designs from other tractor manufacturers.

1949: John Deere Model MC crawler tractors were produced in the Dubuque tractor factory. It was the first all John Deere track-type tractor.

1949: Deere's first diesel-powered tractor, the big John Deere Model R, was introduced. Its hefty engine of 34.27 drawbar hp put the company squarely in the tractor horsepower race.

1950: The Korean War broke out and the United States sent troops to help United Nations forces defend South Korea. Television receivers began to show up in farm homes as new broadcast stations spread their signals across the nation's breadbasket.

1952: The most popular John Deere tractors ever, the Models A and B, were replaced with the more powerful Models 50 and 60. The new tractors boosted power by 15 percent compared to that of the older designs. New styling modernized the Numbered Series that soon grew to include Models 40, 50, 60, 70, and 80.

1953: The John Deere Model 70 replaced the Model G. The following year the 70 was available with diesel or LP gas engine options. Production of the venerable Model D ended its thirty-year run with the assembly of the last "streeters," as Ds built on company streets outside the Waterloo plant became known as.

1954: John Deere revolutionized corn harvesting with its new two-row No. 10 corn head for the No. 45 self-propelled combine. Field-shelling with combines and handling of the corn as shelled grain soon replaced ear corn shucking with its handling of bulky ears. Two years later four-row corn heads were ready for the larger No. 55 combine.

1955: The John Deere Model 80 replaced the R. The 80 boasted a 35 percent increase in horsepower up to 46.32 drawbar hp.

1956: John Deere's new 20 Series of tractors appeared with another 20 percent increase in power for the 420, 520, 620, 720, and 820 models over the Models 40, 50, 60, 70, and 80 they superseded. The new models carried a bold splash of yellow down their hoods for a distinctive new look.

1957: Deere & Company board of directors authorized the building of the modern Deere Administrative Center in a campuslike setting north of the Rock River in Moline. Famed architect Eero Saarinen was chosen to design the center. Deere president William Hewitt's efforts were central to that building's development. It was put into service starting in 1964.

1958: The 20 Series John Deere tractors were replaced with the 30 Series machines which kept the same power plants but added more operator comfort and convenience. The new series also featured areas of yellow trim extending from the hoods down the radiator shroud.

1959: A huge 200-plus-hp, four-wheel-drive Model 8010 John Deere tractor sporting an eight-bottom mounted plow created a sensation at the Marshalltown, Iowa, John Deere fall field day. The big machine didn't fit the usual John Deere tractor two-cylinder mold.

1960: A revolutionary "New Generation of Power" series of John Deere tractors was launched. The completely new 1010, 2010, 3010, and 4010 models sporting their all-new four- and six-cylinder engines caught the spotlight at their gala Dallas, Texas, introduction on August 30. It was a bold move, underway for seven years, that transformed the John Deere machines and helped move Deere & Company to the front in farm tractor sales.

1963: The New Generation models were joined by the wheatland-type John Deere 5010, the industry's first two-wheel-drive tractor with more than 100 horsepower.

1964: The New Generation models were transformed into even more powerful tractors with the introduction of the 3020 and 4020 models. Their new Power Shift transmission gave them eight forward and four reverse speeds shifted by a single lever while the machine was underway and pulling a load. The 4020 soon became the most popular tractor of the day and a classic in its own time.

1965–1969: A total of nine improved New Generation tractor models swelled the long green line, from the smallest, the three-cylinder 31-hp 820 diesel, to the 122.36 PTO hp Turbo-Built 4520 diesel. The latter introduced turbocharging to John Deere tractors.

1971: Intercooling turbocharged air on the John Deere Model 4620 helped it develop 135.76 PTO hp. It was the first farm tractor to use intercooling to supply a denser air flow for turbocharger compressing.

1971: The last of the New Generation series of tractors were introduced. John Deere's first four-wheel-drive row-crop tractors came out in 1971 as the 146.17 PTO hp Model 7020. The bend-in-the-middle machine carried the operator's cab behind the engine on the front drive wheels section of the tractor.

1972: A more powerful version of the big row-crop four-wheel drives, the 7520 with 175.82 PTO hp, was made available. The 6030 was also beefed up and was the largest two-wheel-drive John Deere tractor. It was available as a wheatland-type or with adjustable tread for row-crop work. The 6030, with its 175.99 PTO hp capacity, worked well into the next generation of John Deere tractors. The Deere Generation II tractors, introduced in late 1972, were marked by their innovative Sound-Gard bodies which provided new levels of safety and comfort for tractor operators.

1972–Present: Deere & Company has built on its strengths in the farm equipment field and continues to innovate, expand, and re-engineer its John Deere product line to meet the challenges of agriculture's ever-changing needs.

Carefully tended rows of young corn.

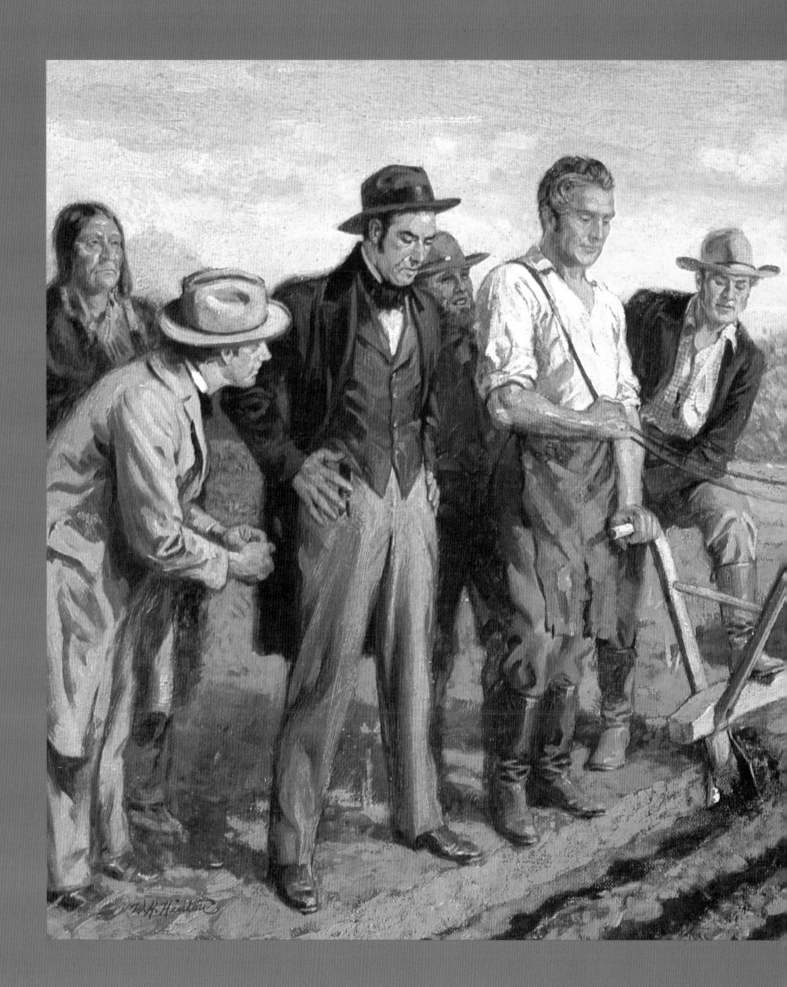

CHAPTER 1

Pre-Tractor Days

Above: *Steady but slow oxen were yoked in pairs for the heavy work on early American farms. The sturdy bovines were gradually replaced by heavy draft horses as new lighter-draft farm equipment was developed.*

Left: *Deere & Company commissioned artist Walter Haskell Hinton to paint a series of images portraying the history of the company. This painting, entitled "His Successful Moment," shows John Deere demonstrating his 1837 plow scouring the sticky Midwestern soil.*

Young blacksmith John Deere at work at his anvil is memorialized in this statue at the John Deere Historic Site in Grand Detour, Illinois. Deere came to the prairie village from Vermont in 1836, with little more in hand than his tools. He had worked as a blacksmith for eleven years after he completed his apprenticeship in Vermont.

John Deere revolutionized agriculture on the American prairies by improving one of the world's oldest agricultural implements, the plow. His plow, hammered out of an old steel sawmill blade, "scoured," or self-polished, in the sticky prairie soils of Illinois, thus solving one of the major problems of tilling the rich prairies and, ultimately, leading to the development of one of the richest agricultural regions on earth, the Corn Belt.

Deere's diligent pursuit of quality and an instinct for marketing helped him grow his one-man plow company into a major maker of farm equipment. His famous self-scouring steel plow of 1837 germinated a company that today carries forward his principles of quality as one of the world's major suppliers of farm implements.

Today's John Deere tractors, which can pull a dozen or more plows through a farm field at a breakneck clip, were impossible to imagine in blacksmith John Deere's world of horse-drawn implements in the first half of the nineteenth century. But the seeds of the Corn Belt and John Deere tractors to plow the fertile land were indeed planted nearly two centuries ago in rural Vermont.

John Deere's Roots

John Deere, the fifth child of a Welsh tailor, William Rinold Deere, and a Connecticut seamstress, Sarah (Yates) Deere, was born February 7, 1804, in Rutland, Vermont. Hard financial times befell John Deere's parents, and, in 1808, when John was only four, William set sail for England to collect an inheritance, but he was lost at sea and never returned. The responsibility of raising the family fell to Sarah. To support her children, she took up the tailoring business where her husband had left off.

When he was seventeen, John Deere apprenticed to blacksmith Captain Benjamin Lawrence of Middlebury, Vermont. In addition to his training in blacksmithing, Deere was to receive instruction in mathematics, writing, and reading. His room, board, and clothing were included. For his efforts in helping the blacksmith during his apprenticeship, Deere received a stipend of thirty dollars the first year, which increased by five dollars per year as he progressed through the training and became a more proficient apprentice. Deere completed his apprenticeship and began work as a journeyman blacksmith in 1825.

Deere worked in several towns in Vermont, including Vergennes, Salisbury, Royalton, Hancock, and Leicester, where he had his own shop. But by late 1836, John Deere was struggling. His recurrent bad luck included two fires that burned out his fledgling smithing shop in Leicester. Those fires plunged him deeply in debt to a silent partner, Jay Wright, who had loaned Deere money for his first blacksmith shop in 1831. After the fires, Wright began pressing Deere for immediate payment.

Not on its original location, but guided in its re-creation by archeological input, John Deere's re-created shop today shows Grand Detour visitors the kind of tools Deere used in 1837 to create his famous self-scouring plow.

Deere's options were limited. He couldn't pay the debt and the alternatives were ominous. He was faced with the embarrassment of bankruptcy or even the possibility of imprisonment as a debtor, under Vermont laws of the day, if he didn't satisfy Wright's claim.

In addition, serious economic pressures in his native state were plaguing Deere and other blacksmiths and businesses. By 1836, Vermont's agriculture had become mostly a monoculture of sheep and wool production, according to Wayne G. Broehl, Jr., in his 1984 tome, *John Deere's Company: A History of Deere & Company and Its Times*. With the majority of the land in the state devoted to sheep pasture, crop farming had shrunk to a minimum. Small farms were being bought up by the relatively affluent wool growers. That meant fewer crop farms and, consequently, a shrinking demand for tillage implements and hand tools—Deere's specialty. It all added up to less work for the many blacksmiths in the area. By the following year the financial panic of 1837 was in full bloom, and money was extremely scarce. Times were bad.

Facing such difficult economic factors and Wright's active debt collection effort, Deere decided to leave Vermont. In the fall of 1836, the young blacksmith made his lone way west, drawn by the promise of a fresh start to better provide for his family. He left his wife, Demarius, then six months pregnant, and their four other children behind in Hancock, Vermont, where they could be near her parents, and John headed for the tiny pioneer village of Grand Detour, Illinois, a mere speck of a place 100 miles (160 km) due west of Chicago on the Rock River and more than 1,200 miles (1,920 km) from his Vermont roots.

THE BLACKSMITH MEETS THE PRAIRIE

The Erie Canal, from Albany to Buffalo, New York, had been completed in 1825. For many Easterners, the canal provided access to the burgeoning Midwest via the Great Lakes, and, about ten years after the canal opened, settlement in northern Illinois began in earnest. John Deere was among this first wave of settlers, and he later recalled that he made his long journey to Grand Detour by canal boat, lake boat, and stagecoach.

Grand Detour, named for its location inside a looping double oxbow in the Rock River, was surrounded by vast prairies growing rank with mixed species of tall native grasses and other plants. Though predominantly grasses, the prairie vegetation was diverse with more than 270 different plant species. Historian Allan G. Bogue, in his book, *From Prairie to Corn Belt,* says observers of the 1830–1850s referred to the prairies as a "vast ocean of meadow-land."

Deere, it is said, arrived on the plains with little more than his smithing tools. Some stories say he had but $73.73 to his name when he got to Grand Detour. He immediately went to work mending farm equipment, wagons, and stagecoaches, as well as shoeing horses and making shovels, hoes, and pitchforks.

Vermonters Leonard Andrus and his cousins Willis T. and Willard A. House were already at work in Grand De-

tour when Deere arrived. They had traveled west in 1835, and, by the time John Deere showed up, they had already harnessed the Rock River to power a sawmill and gristmill and had built log homes for their own families. Andrus was later to become a Deere partner in the plow-making business.

Lore has it that one of Deere's first tasks was to repair a broken pitman shaft on the Leonard Andrus sawmill—a job that required a temporary forge to be built in short order. The pitman shaft moved the saw blade up and down. Deere was up to the challenge; he built the forge and had the sawmill back in operation in a couple of days.

PRAIRIES CAME ON THE WIND

Unlike the often rocky, sometimes sandy, and usually shallow and light-colored forest soils of the eastern United States, the deep virgin Illinois prairie soils had been formed on the treeless plains under long-rooted grasses in the ten thousand years or so since the last glacial advance and retreat. These black, high-organic-content soils were developed from the thick layers of loess, or glacial silt, blown upland from the glacial floodplains in the nearby river bottoms.

Over thousands of years of weathering by nature's forces, the prairie soils had become rich with black organic matter, or humus. Organic matter accumulated in the prairie soils to a great depth from the annual growth and decay of the tall prairie vegetation. That build-up was stirred deep by burrowing animals, including prairie dogs, groundhogs, and others. The soils covered by forests, on the other hand, where trees might live as long as a century or so before completing their life cycle of growth and decay, were deprived of the build-up of organic matter made possible on the prairie. So, forest soils were lighter colored, shallower, and held less organic matter and native fertility.

In the 1830s, new settlers to the prairie were just discovering the potential of the deep, black, fertile soils under the tangled heavy mat of grass and other prairie plants. Many settlers arriving after 1835 found little but prairie land left on which to settle, as most

As many as 270 identified plant species gave great variety and beauty to the prairie vegetation. These blooms brighten a restored prairie planted with native species at the John Deere Historic Site.

woodlands were already occupied. Some families, forced to accept prairie ground in their land purchases, tackled the difficult task of plowing and planting where no trees grew. They were amazed at their yields from the prairie soil. The previously held belief among the Easterners was that if the prairie didn't grow trees, it couldn't grow crops. But periodic prairie fires, either started by lightning or set by Native Americans to herd game or to clear garden tracts, were the main reason the prairies were not covered with trees. The racing prairie fires' flames seared tree seedlings and stopped them from spreading up ravines and across the plains. These fires, fueled by residue from the thick prairie vegetation, effectively created the tree-free prairies by confining tree growth to low, wet areas near streams.

The prairie settlers soon realized that the vast plains of the Midwest were indeed fertile—but not easy to plow and plant. Early trials of prairie cropping proved fruitful but difficult. Settlers planting both forest and prairie soils could see the difference: The thin forest soils soon "wore out" after a few seasons of crops, while the deep prairie soils kept up their high level of output year after year. Once the prairie soil was recognized for its wealth of fertility, "breaking," or turning under, the sod in preparation for tilling and planting became the first challenge for the settlers. Keeping it cultivated was the ever-continuing job.

Breaking the heavy sod allowed the mass of roots and vegetation to deteriorate so cropping could start. Much of the needed initial sod breaking was actually hired out as custom work at $2 to $4 per acre to operators who used huge (by the standards of the day) cart-mounted 16 to 24-inch (41–61-cm) single-bottom sod-breaking plows pulled by from four to six plodding oxen. By contrast, the land itself in that part of Illinois sold for around $1.25 per acre. Some farmers did their own sod breaking with smaller plows and smaller hitches of either oxen or horses.

"The first plowing of the sod, ordinarily referred to as 'breaking prairie', was in its way an arduous undertaking," remembered Charles B. Johnson, M.D., in *Illinois in the Fifties,* his 1918 book about growing up on a farm in Bond County, Illinois, in the 1850s. Johnson recalled the sod breaking: "The usual outfit for this was a large, strong plow drawn by oxen. Immediately in front of the point of the plow was a coulter, a strong piece of iron securely fastened to the beam and provided with a sharp cutting edge, which divided the sod turned over from that remaining. As a result of this arrangement, the turned-over sod was of a uniform width and thickness. Six yoke [or pairs] of oxen not infrequently comprised the propelling power of one of these plows which opened a furrow two feet [61 cm] or more in width, and cut roots, and any ordinary obstruction, with the utmost facility. This plow, like all others of its time, had handles, but in addition was attached by its beam to a pair of low wheels which held it steady and kept it from turning over." In a good day such an outfit could break up to two acres (0.8 ha) of prairie.

"The man who drove the oxen, the ox-driver, was a unique character," Johnson continues. "He was coarse, rough, had a loud voice and could 'swear by note' when the emergency seemed to demand it. He carried a long, heavy ox-whip, the insignia, as it were, of his calling. It was made of twisted raw-hide, in its thickest part was an inch [2.5 cm] in diameter, and was attached to a long handle made from a small, growing hickory upon which the bark remained. This whip he was fond of flourishing and cracking with a sharp report, and meantime any laggard in the team was sure to get from it a prompt stroke. For each of his oxen he had names and when they were pulling the plow he was constantly directing this one, correcting that one, and chiding the other. It was 'Gee, Buck!' 'Haw, Bright!' 'Git up, Baldy!' 'What are you doing there, Spot!' and so on till none were slighted either with voice or whiplash."

"When the prairie sod was turned over in the spring it was at once planted in corn," Johnson recalled. "This was usually done with a hoe (sometimes with an ax), and as the growing crop required, and received no cultivation, it was known as 'sod-corn.'"

STICKY SOIL AND THE DEERE SOLUTION

It was in the years following the sod breaking and the early crops of sod corn that the new prairie farmers first ran into a "sticky" problem. As the last remnants of the prairie vegetation decomposed, the heavy, black gumbo stuck to their cast-iron or iron-covered wooden plowshares and moldboards. Thus "gummed up" with sticky soil, the moldboards wouldn't turn over the soil but merely pushed it aside, with the plow coming out of the ground in the process. No matter how often they were scraped and scoured with paddles or blades, the sticky soil would cling again to the plow bottom's porous cast-iron surfaces just as soon as the plow went back into the ground. Trying to plow under those conditions was painfully slow—if not impossible. Some early settlers despaired of ever getting the prairie to "work" and moved on to more promising areas of the country that didn't have the troublesome sticky prairie soils.

In this painting by Walter Haskell Hinton, blacksmith John Deere displays his self-scouring plow amongst a progression of explorers, settlers, and farmers depicting the development of the Corn Belt.

The enterprising blacksmith from the East soon learned from his farmer customers that there was a crying need for a plowshare and moldboard that would polish to a smooth surface and scour itself. That would allow the heavy soil to slide off the metal as the plow sheared off a slice of earth and turned it over. There had been at least one earlier attempt at using steel to solve the problem. In 1831, John Lane of Lockport, Illinois, also a blacksmith, used part of a broken saw blade to make a plow with a steel share and moldboard. His plow was not a commercial success.

In 1837, John Deere also took part of a broken steel sawmill blade, cut off the teeth with a chisel, heated the one-time saw in his forge, hammered it over a piece of wood into a curved diamond-shaped plow, mounted it into a frame with a massive wooden beam for pulling it, and fitted handles formed from saplings with the curves of the roots for handholds. The steel, probably from a

vertical, straight jig-type saw of the era and likely from the Andrus mill (since it was the only sawmill in Grand Detour), may already have been polished to a near mirror surface from its numerous up and down strokes through Ogle and Lee Counties, oak, black walnut, maple, and elm.

Deere tested his crude steel plow on a farm just across the Rock River from Grand Detour, in a field that had the requisite sticky soil to prove his concept. It worked! Hitched to neighbor Lewis Crandall's horses with Deere handling the steering, the plow scoured on its own and turned over the heavy black soil in "long greasy ribbons," according to reports of the day.

The good news spread, and demand for the plows grew. John Deere was soon busy at his forge hammering out and then polishing his steel plows, first as a solitary venture in his own shop, then with a series of partners. Deere approached his market differently than had other early

Company founder, John Deere, was president of corporate Deere & Company from 1868 until his death at eighty-two in 1886. He was born in Vermont in 1804. (Deere & Company archives)

John Deere's home in Grand Detour, Illinois, was started by Deere soon after he arrived in 1836. John's wife, Demarius, and their five Vermont-born children, joined the plow maker in Grand Detour in 1838 and lived in this house. Begun as a small 18x24-foot (5.5x7.3-m) 1½-story cottage, additions were made as the Deere family grew. It was the Deere home until they moved to Moline in 1848. Deere & Company restored it in 1962 and furnished it with period pieces.

farm tool makers. Instead of waiting for orders to come to him at the shop, he made his plows and then went out and sold them on approval. Deere later recalled making two plows in 1838, ten more in 1839, forty in 1840, seventy-five in 1841, and one hundred in 1842, all sold by the same method.

DEERE IS JOINED BY HIS FAMILY

Soon after he arrived in Grand Detour in 1836 and before he made his first steel plow in 1837, John Deere built a modest, five-room, one-and-a-half-story frame house of about 18x24 feet (5.5x7.3 m) just west of his blacksmith shop. It included a fireplace in the living room and had a steep stairway to two upstairs bedrooms. The Deere home and blacksmith shop, as restored by Deere & Company in the 1960s, can be visited today in Grand Detour. It was only the second frame home erected in the village; almost all earlier buildings were log structures.

By 1838, Deere was ready for his family to join him in Illinois. His wife, Demarius, and their five young children traveled to Grand Detour by wagon with Demarius's sister Lucretia and husband, John Peek, and their children. The youngest Deere, Charles, had been born in Vermont in March 1837 and made the six-week trek to Illinois as a toddler. Charles was destined to carry his father's company forward into the next Deere generation. The older children were Francis, born in 1828; Jeanette, born in 1830; Ellen, born in 1832; and Frances, born in 1834.

Five more children were born to John and Demarius in Illinois. Emma, born in 1840; Hiram, born in 1842; Alice, born in 1844; an unnamed baby stillborn in 1845; and Mary, born in 1851. Of the ten, only five, Jeanette, Ellen, Charles, Emma, and Alice, lived to maturity and married.

By 1843, Deere's twelve-year-old past-due notes to Jay Wright from Vermont caught up to him. Debts to Wright,

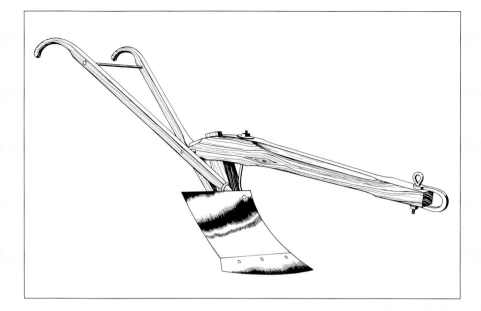

Smithsonian Institution historians in Washington, D.C., think this is the probable construction of John Deere's 1838 plow. The drawing is based on the remains of an 1838 plow it received from Deere & Company in 1938. (Deere & Company archives)

The Smithsonian Plow

In 1901, what were believed to be the remains, missing only its handles, of one of the two plows Deere made in 1838 were still on the farm of the original buyer, Joseph Brierton, a few miles south of Grand Detour. That year, Charles Deere, John Deere's son and then-president of Deere & Company, obtained the plow.

The early plow was exhibited in the Deere offices for many years. Then, in 1938, a century after it was made by John Deere, Deere & Company presented the plow to the Smithsonian Institution in Washington, D.C. There, Edward C. Kendall, curator of agriculture in the institution's Museum of History and Technology, carefully studied the plow. Metallurgical analysis showed the moldboard was of wrought iron and the share was steel. Kendall concluded from his observations that the successful prairie plow with a smooth one-piece moldboard and steel share was basically Deere's idea. He noted that the moldboards of practically all of Deere's plows produced from 1837 to 1852 were made of wrought iron rather than steel. Kendall concluded that the importance attached to the sharp-edged and highly polished steel share, to which the sticky prairie soil would not cling, led to the plows being called "steel" plows.

Kendall wrote a paper about the plow stating, "The Museum's John Deere plow is a very early specimen, on the basis of a comparison of it with Deere moldboards of 1847 and 1855 and its conformity to Deere's description of his plows in an 1843 advertisement; and the 1838 date associated with it is plausible."

The 1843 ad that Kendall referred to appeared in the February 3, 1843, issue of the *Rock River Register,* a weekly in Grand Detour. The ad describes a plow for sale under the headline "Patent Cary Plow." The ad announced: "John Deere respectfully informs his friends and customers, the agricultural community, of this and the adjoining counties, and dealers in Ploughs, that he is now prepared to fill orders for the same on presentation. The mouldboard of this well, and

so favorably known plough, is made of wrought iron, and the share of steel, 5-16 of an inch [80 mm] thick, which carries a fine sharp edge. The whole face of the mouldboard and share is ground smooth, so that it scours perfectly bright in any soil, and will not choke in the foulest of ground. It will do more work in a day, and do it much better and with less labor, to both team and holder, than the ordinary ploughs that do not scour, and in consequence of the ground being better prepared, the agriculturalist obtains a much heavier crop."

But modern-day business chronicler Wayne G. Broehl, Jr., points out in his *John Deere's Company* that the Patent Cary (also known as the Dagen) plow was made by prominent Illinois plow maker Jewett & Hitchcock of Springfield. The Patent Cary plow was originally made in Connecticut, according to Broehl, and was being made in the East by others in a rather standardized form. Jewett's improvement was the attachment of the share with rivets. Around the same time that Deere's 1843 ad appeared, Jewett & Hitchcock were advertising their plow all over the state as "Jewett's Improved Patent Cary Plow." Their own ads stated similarly that *"The moldboard of this so well and so favorably known plow is made of wrought iron, 5/16 of an inch [80 mm] thick, and the share of steel which carries a fine edge, the whole face of the moldboard and share is ground smooth, so that it scours perfectly bright in any soil and will not choke in the foulest ground."* It sounds like it's the same plow in both ads. The ad placed by John Deere suggests that he was selling the Jewett-made plow at least in 1842 and 1843, as were other makers and merchants. Whether those sales of the Jewett-made plows count against the one hundred plows "made" by John Deere in 1842 and the four hundred in 1843 is unknown. Perhaps John Deere's production of his own plow couldn't meet the demand for plows, and he helped fill that gap by selling the Springfield-made Patent Cary plow. The mystery remains to this day.

by then amounting to $1,000, with accumulated interest and court costs, were the subject of an Ogle County (Illinois) Circuit Court case that year naming John Deere defendant. Deere must have settled the debt at that time because the case was dismissed by agreement of the parties, with the defendant paying the court costs, according to Ogle County records as reported by Broehl in his book.

In 1846, John Deere and his partner, Leonard Andrus, built this two-story plow factory on the banks of the Rock River about a block northeast of Deere's original shop in Grand Detour, Illinois. In 1847, the Grand Detour partnership began to falter, and, in 1848, Deere moved his plow-making enterprise to Moline, Illinois. (Deere & Company archives)

PLOW PARTNERS

John Deere and his neighbors in Grand Detour must have heard opportunity knocking in the rattling of wagon wheels as more and more settlers came west to the prairies. All around their growing village in Illinois the prairie was being taken up by settlers, many of them fellow Yankees from New England. Leonard Andrus, a fellow Vermonter and owner of a sawmill (where John Deere likely found the broken sawmill blade he used to make the first steel-shared plow), was to play another role in John Deere's enterprise. In early 1843, entrepreneur Andrus became a Deere partner in plow making. Their Grand Detour partnership first operated as L. Andrus & Company.

It was reported that L. Andrus & Company made four hundred plows in 1843, after improvements were made to Deere's blacksmith shop. However, Deere also advertised that year to sell what was probably the Patent Cary plow made by Jewett & Hitchcock, so the actual number of Deere plows made in 1843 remains uncertain.

In 1844, another partner joined them, a local merchant named Horace Paine. But by 1846, Paine was gone, and Andrus and Deere took in Oramil C. Lathrop as a partner. Also in 1846, they built a two-story "Plough Manufactory" on the Rock River, about a block northeast of Deere's blacksmith shop, equipped it, and got even more serious about plow making. The new steam-powered plant helped them double plow production. They operated as Andrus, Deere & Lathrop until June 22, 1847, when Lathrop apparently dropped out, and the partnership briefly became Andrus & Deere. By then they were making one thousand plows per year. But major changes were in the offing.

MOLINE MOVE

In May 1848, five years after their partnership began, Andrus and Deere parted ways. Deere accepted $1,200 from Andrus for his half interest in the partnership, and Deere likely also got a customer list for half of their trade, some of which consisted of a list of plows sold on credit. Deere then relocated his operation downriver about sixty miles (97 km), to Moline, Illinois, near the junction of the Rock and Mississippi Rivers, where the Mississippi bends to flow west for about thirty miles (49 km).

Back in Grand Detour, Leonard Andrus continued to make plows with his brother-in-law, Colonel Amos Bosworth II. The Andrus firm continued with other partners and eventually became the Grand Detour Plow Company. In 1869, the plow maker moved to nearby Dixon. The J. I. Case Threshing Machine Company of Racine, Wisconsin, purchased the Grand Detour Plow Company in 1919 to add plows to its own equipment line, thus laying claim to some of the early steel plow history. J. I. Case Company, drawing on its acquired Andrus heritage, celebrated one hundred years in plow making in 1937 at the same time Deere & Company celebrated the very same milestone.

THE MOLINE PLOW WORKS

Moline, named for its flour and sawmills (the town's name is an adaptation of the French *moulin,* meaning "mill"), had been settled in 1832, and it was still a frontier village when Deere arrived in 1848. But he recognized that it held more promise as a manufacturing site than did Grand Detour. Water power and the availability of steam-powered river transportation at Moline must have been powerful incentives for the move. At Grand Detour, everything from coal to power the steam engines to the plows themselves had to be shipped by wagon over forty miles (65 km) of muddy trails. Steamships generally could not reach the town on the shallow Rock River. By 1847, John Deere knew

JOHN DEERE'S PLOW WORKS. 1847.

A new Deere partnership of Deere, Tate, & Gould, began making John Deere Moline Centre-Draft Plows at this new plow works on the banks of the Mississippi River at Moline, Illinois, in 1848. The plant was in production by September 1848, just five months after Deere moved his business to Moline. The new factory was marked with the wrong date of establishment, but for his own reasons John Deere let the 1847 date stand. (Deere & Company archives)

Grand Detour was to be bypassed by the railroads, leaving it without adequate water or rail transportation to support the scale of business he envisioned.

In Moline, Deere formed a new partnership with Robert N. Tate, an Englishman who had previously worked with Deere to install steam power at the Grand Detour Plough Manufactory and to update some of the company's machinery. Under the new partnership, Tate served as foreman, and, with his direction, a factory was quickly erected in Moline. By September 1848, just five months after the move from Grand Detour, the Deere & Tate partnership was making plows in their new 24x60-foot (7.3x18.3-m) plant on the east bank of the Mississippi River. It was located near the chute in the river formed by the narrow passage just upriver from Rock Island on the Illinois side—an ideal location. A company ad from about 1850–1852 boasted: "As we have unlimited water power—are in the immediate vicinity of inexhaustible beds of bituminous coal and in continual receipt of the best lumber of the upper regions of Iowa and Wisconsin (three very important considerations), we are enabled to execute all branches of our business, in the most durable and substantial manner, and CHEAPER than the same quality of work can be executed in any other location in the country."

John M. Gould, a business friend of Deere from Grand Detour, signed on as another partner that fall of 1848, and the new Moline firm became Deere, Tate & Gould. Starting as a clerk in 1844 at the Grand Detour depart-

ment store of Dana and Troop, Gould had risen to partner in that firm. His skills as a bookkeeper were particularly valuable to the fledgling plow company. Gould became the manager of finance.

John Deere, apparently left the shop in Tate's care, and he and Gould started traveling to market Deere's self-scouring plow. Their efforts soon paid off, and the reputation of John Deere's plow spread. Farm newsletter *Prairie Farmer*, reported in its March 1851 issue: "*The Grand de Tour Plow*: About 10 years ago a Mr. Deere commenced the making of a plow with the above name, which soon became celebrated in all the Rock River region, and for a considerable distance up and down the Mississippi. This plow, with improvements, is still manufactured by the original inventor, or one of the firm of Deere, Tate & Gould, at Moline, the call for it having been greatly extended. Cast-steel mould-boards, made by Noyes & Co., of Sheffield, England, are now used. The implement is now named the 'Moline Center Draft Plow.'"

In the first five months of 1849, the plow works turned out 1,200 plows, and Deere and his partners expanded the factory with a two-story, 30x80-foot (9.1x24.4-m) addition. By 1852, Deere, Tate & Gould was making 4,000 plows a year and had added an early grain drill, the Seymour, to their line. Evidently farmers were too accustomed to broadcasting their seed by hand, or using a neck-slung cyclone or horn seeder, to justify paying eighty dollars for the Seymour. Grain drill sales were sluggish, and the Seymour was soon dropped from the Deere, Tate & Gould product line.

THE END OF DEERE, TATE & GOULD

In 1852, the three partners decided to go their separate ways. Charged with the responsibilities of plow production, Tate was apparently rankled by Deere's constant tinkering with the plows. Deere's goal, of course, was to make the plows even better, to produce a constantly improving plow. "If we don't improve our product, somebody else will beat us and we will lose our trade," Deere is said to have insisted. Tate, on the other hand, wanted to "freeze" the design and concentrate instead on production and selling farmers the plows as produced.

Gould also had some dissatisfaction with the arrangement. He apparently became weary of trying to make long term credit receivables cover short term expense payables, as he was forced to juggle them in their plow business.

Divided by these issues, Deere, Tate, and Gould agreed to dissolve the partnership; Tate and Gould left the company. Tate became a Deere competitor four years later in 1856 when he and Charles Buford, along with Buford's son Bassett, formed a full-line plow company called Buford and Tate. That business was the foundation of what later became the Rock Island Plow Company. Gould started a wooden ware company called Dimock and Gould. The company's pails, tubs, and other items of wood were sold to merchants for cash. He later established a banking firm in Moline named Gould, Dimock & Company.

Despite the dissolution of the partnership, John Deere, as Deere's plow works was now called, continued to thrive. In 1855, the Deere plow took first prize at the Illinois State Fair, and the growing company was making thirteen different kinds of plow, "turning them off at the rate of 35 a day and for the coming year intended to get off 10,000," *Prairie Farmer* reported.

Between 1853 and 1857, John Deere's annual plow production more than tripled to 13,400 units. By 1854, John Deere's son Charles was working for his father and soon became head salesman.

John Deere advertised nine different models of Moline Plows in 1857 in what was now called its "Clipper" line, varying in size from 12 to 14 inches (30.5–35.6 cm) in cutting width. The company continued to produce breaker plows for turning sod, as well as an emerging line of cultivators, harrows, and other horse-drawn tillage equipment.

FINANCIAL CRISIS AVERTED

Reorganization of the plow company came once more in 1857, brought on by cash-flow problems caused by the financial panic of that year. Prices of farm products dropped steeply. Not surprisingly, farmers quit paying their notes to John Deere dealers, who in turn could not pay Deere.

At the same time, Deere had a hefty debt to suppliers for the iron, steel, and wood already made into implements. As receivables continued to shrink, the situation for John Deere became precarious.

On July 1, 1857, Deere's son-in-law James Chapman, a lawyer, stepped in and assembled a deal to set up a new partnership of "John Deere & Company" with partners John Deere, Charles Deere, Luke Hemenway, and David H. Bugbee. Hemenway had been a Deere partner briefly in Grand Detour in 1841–1842 and had joined Deere as chief bookkeeper in Moline in 1855. Bugbee was also a Deere employee. They were considered temporary partners, though they received salaries during the life of the partnership. By March 1858, the crisis had been averted, and, with shored-up lines of credit in place, the brief partnership was ended, and John Deere again became sole proprietor, according to historian Broehl. Hemenway and Bugbee were given back their partnership contributions, and Charles Deere gave his father long-term notes for the elder Deere's interests, effectively buying control. That

John Deere Centre-Draft plow advertisement from 1854. (Deere & Company archives)

Charles Deere, corporate president of Deere & Company from 1886 to his death in 1907 at the age of seventy, was born in Vermont in March 1837, after his father John Deere had moved to Grand Detour, Illinois. (Deere & Company archives)

Travelers Lead the Life

Once the plows were made, polished, assembled, painted, and carefully stenciled with the John Deere name, they had to be shipped and sold. Here, the river also played a pivotal role.

Travelers, as Deere's traveling salesmen were called, rode the steamships to make their plow-selling and debt-collecting rounds up and down the Mississippi and other major rivers of the Great Plains. Mark Twain, in his celebrated *Life on the Mississippi*, quoted the enthusiasm of one such salesman, "You show me any country under the sun where they really know how to plow, and if I don't show you our mark on the plow they use, I'll eat the plow, and I won't ask for any 'Woostershyre' sauce to flavor it up with, either." The salesman could have been a John Deere traveler.

Deere travelers ventured by steamship up the Mississippi to Dubuque, Iowa; Galena, Illinois; Prairie du Chien, Wisconsin; and, eventually, St. Anthony, Minnesota, part of present-day Minneapolis. Downriver shipping points were Burlington and Keokuk, Iowa; Quincy, Illinois; St. Louis; and even New Orleans and the Gulf of Mexico. The travelers could peddle their wares as far as Pittsburgh via the Ohio River, Peoria via the Illinois River, and even all the way upstream on the Missouri to Fort Benton, Montana. It became even more apparent now that Moline was an ideal location.

In 1854, the Chicago & Rock Island Railroad reached Moline, providing needed rail connections to the east, south, and north, and greatly enhancing the shipping possibilities for Deere's company. In 1856, the first railroad bridge over the Mississippi, just downriver from Moline between Rock Island, Illinois, and Davenport, Iowa, let the rails stretch westward.

Once the implements arrived at the riverbank landings or rail depots, in an era when informal business arrangements prevailed, teamsters with their heavy, horse-drawn wagons loaded the plows on wagons, delivered them into the country to customers previously contacted by travelers, and sometimes sold them one or two at a time for cash to individual farmers. The teamsters were independent contractors. Any surplus plows at the end of their run were typically sold to general merchandisers in farm towns, as Deere didn't want plows returned. Gradually, an informal dealership system evolved with the general merchandisers selling the John Deere plows on credit and then reimbursing Deere when they were paid by the farmers after the crops were harvested. The travelers apparently handled the collection of the receipts for Deere, less the dealers' commissions. The credit arrangements complicated the sale of plows but assisted farmers in paying for them, ultimately resulting in better sales.

In some rural areas, the crossroads country store became the local outlet for John Deere's implements. When the weather first showed promise of the coming of spring, the farmer could go to the country store for one-stop buying to get "geared-up" for the plowing and planting season. In many cases the merchant, already providing credit to his customers for groceries and other supplies, wrote up notes for the Deere equipment and also carried them on his books, then collected for the good and implements and plow parts after crops were harvested and sold. As with the regular dealers, travelers also collected for the John Deere machines from these outlets.

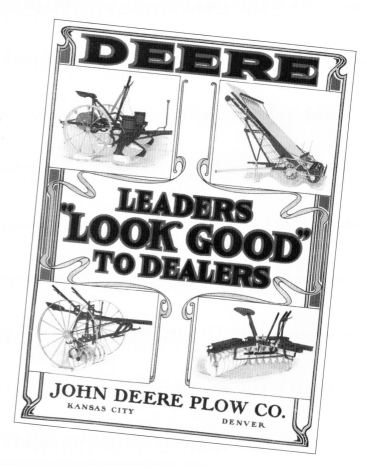

A late-1800s ad features some of the Deere products distributed by travelers and later sold through branch houses.

placed active control of the company in Charles Deere's hands. Charles, at the age of twenty-one, became largely responsible for the day-to-day management of the company. John Deere, then fifty-eight, remained personally involved with the firm but apparently played a reduced role in overall management. This arrangement let the elder Deere return to the shop and continue his real passion: hands-on product improvement and process development.

PROSPERITY ON THE PRAIRIES IN THE FACE OF WAR

The Civil War in the early 1860s created a boom in the emerging prairie states. Farms in the area were called upon to increase production to meet the demands of the Civil War to feed, clothe, shoe, and move the Union armies. Already exporting a lot of its corn and pork to the southern states, Midwest farmers more than made up for the loss of that market by increased sales to the federal government. Not only were corn and meat needed by the government in large amounts, but so was leather for soldiers' boots, as well as for harnesses to outfit the increasing numbers of mule and horse teams needed to move troops, supplies, and munitions.

In addition, the demand for raw wool soared. Textile production, quickly adjusting to the shortage of cotton from the South, turned increasingly to wool, creating a lively market for raw wool and greatly increasing the number and size of sheep flocks grazing in Midwestern farm fields. By the middle of 1862, a little over a year after the beginning of the Civil War, prosperity in the northern states had soared to unprecedented levels.

Deere and other farm implement makers also helped alleviate the crippling manpower shortage on northern farms due to the war's demand for soldiers. Perfected machines, including improved plows, corn planters, two-horse cultivators, mowers, reapers, and threshing machines, permitted increased labor productivity on farms in the face of fewer farm workers.

The elimination of ox yokes from the John Deere equipment catalog of 1862 suggests the important changes taking place in farm implements and farm production methods at that time. Lighter draft implements for tillage and cultivation helped replace the plodding ox of frontier America with the much swifter and more agile horse and mule.

During the war, farms expanded in the Midwest following the arrival of the railroad. By 1864, improved farm equipment enabled the ordinary farmer to expand his operation from about forty acres (16 ha) of crops per farm to nearly seventy acres (28 ha) on average.

DEERE & COMPANY DURING THE CIVIL WAR

The new farm prosperity of the 1860s impacted John Deere & Company, fortuitously situated in Moline, Illinois, at the very heart of the expanding food belt. However, the decade started poorly for Deere. In November 1860, the Deere & Company partnership between Charles Deere and brother-in-law Christopher C. Webber, which had formed in late 1858, was dissolved with but $60,000 in questionable receivables. Credit reporters of the day thought those receivables might bring but ten cents on the dollar. But Charles Deere continued the company alone as the Moline Plow Manufactory, and the credit reviews got better and better as each year of the war passed. By December 1866, the credit review firm of R. G. Dun &

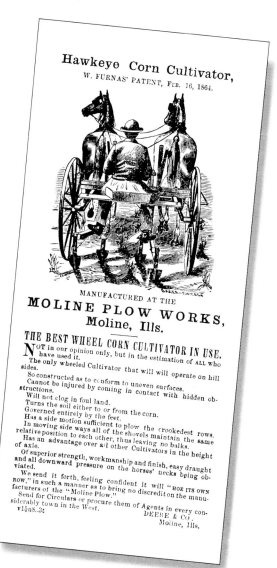

John Deere first put a seat on one of its machines when it began to make its Hawkeye Corn Cultivator, also known as the Hawkeye Riding (Sulky) Cultivator, in 1863 under a patent agreement with inventor W. Furnas. Advertisements proclaimed that it would "Hoe its own row."

Company reported Deere's credit was "First class. Rich!"

During the war a seller's market existed, and the company could, and did, demand cash for its products. The 1862 catalog showed price increases ranging from $.75 to $2.00 per cataloged implement. As Deere chronicler Wayne G. Broehl, Jr., observed in his 1984 book, "The company did very well indeed during the Civil War."

In July 1864, the firm again became Deere & Company with John and Charles Deere as equal partners. They each contributed $70,000 in stock, buildings, and machinery, and collectable notes for implements already sold.

Charles continued to have the primary role in management, and his father continued his tinkering in the shop. In 1864, John Deere received the company's first patent for a process improvement related to casting steel plows.

Another innovation of this time period, though one not unique to Deere & Company, was the riding cultivator. The Hawkeye Riding (Sulky) Cultivator was added to the John Deere product line in 1863, the first John Deere machine with a seat. It was made by Deere under a patent agreement with inventor W. Furnas but was marked with the John Deere name. Sales of the labor-saving machine reached 500 units in 1864 and bloomed to 2,000 cultivators sold in 1865. The sulky concept, meaning the operator rode instead of walked, was about to spread to other John Deere machines.

DEERE & COMPANY INCORPORATES AND BRANCHES OUT

Deere & Company was incorporated in 1868, ending the long parade of John Deere partnerships tracing back to the company's Grand Detour days. Deere began its corporate life August 15, 1868, as Deere & Company with a capitalization consisting of $105,000 in buildings and $45,265 in machinery and equipment. The four original shareholders were John Deere with 25 percent of the stock as president and Charles Deere with 40 percent as vice-president, as well as smaller holdings for John Deere's son-in-law Stephen H. Velie and his nephew George W. Vinton. In 1869, two others became shareholders: Charles V. Nason, also a Deere relative and the superintendent of wood work and the paint shop at the company, and Gilpin Moore, the superintendent of iron works and the only shareholder not related to the Deere family.

In its first year of incorporated operation, the company sold more than 41,000 plows, harrows, and cultivators.

The year 1869 also marked the establishment of the first Deere branch house in Kansas City, Missouri. Deere branch houses were initially separately capitalized, semi-autonomous distribution companies aimed at decentralizing some of the firm's marketing efforts. They operated like wholesale outlets to supply farm equipment dealers and service accounts in each branch's territory. Existing outlets were typically acquired by the Deere interests to start the branches. In later years, Deere & Company bought and owned the branch houses outright.

The new branch houses helped Deere broaden the scope of products the company would later produce. The branch houses and dealer organizations were early sources of ideas for new and improved products that could better serve farmers.

The Kansas City branch house was opened under a partnership between Charles Deere and Alvah Mansur, an eastern businessman who had worked with Deere for a couple of years just before the Civil War. The Kansas City branch prospered, and, in 1875, Mansur moved to St. Louis and helped open a branch there, also in partnership with Deere.

Deere had previously sold through wholesaler William Koenig & Company in St. Louis. The 1875 Koenig catalog lists ten models of Deere plows ranging from 6½-inch to 16-inch (16.5–40.6-cm) cutting widths. Prices on those plows ranged from $9.25 for the small 6½-inch (16.5-cm) "one horse plow" up to $20 for the 16-inch (40.6-cm) "three horse plow." The famous Hawkeye Riding (Sulky) Cultivator was available from Koenig for $40.

The Minneapolis branch was established in 1880 based on the Christian & Dean agricultural equipment house there. C. C. Webber, son of Charles Deere's brother-in-law and former partner, Christopher C. Webber, joined the branch in 1881.

The Omaha branch was started at Council Bluffs, Iowa, in 1881 as Deere, Wells & Company. In 1889, it moved across the Missouri River to Omaha, Nebraska.

California and the West joined in the Deere marketing effort in 1889 when the Deere Implement Company was organized in San Francisco, utilizing part of the former Marcus C. Hawley hardware and agricultural house.

THE GILPIN SULKY PLOW

Meanwhile back in Moline, Gilpin Moore had been innovating. The result was the 1875 Gilpin Sulky Plow, which had roots in the 1863 Hawkeye Riding (Sulky) Cultivator. The two-wheel Gilpin Sulky Plow not only allowed the driver to sit and plow, but gave him a lever with which to accurately set the plow depth. It was not an industry first, but it was a good design. It had a hefty, iron-beam construction with its wooden parts all bound in iron. By 1879, the Gilpin Sulky Plow was metal throughout.

Incidentally, it was in this era that Deere first began to use the leaping deer as a trademark symbol for the company. Several different versions of the deer, which at first was shown leaping over a log, have appeared since 1876. In the mid-1890s, Charles Deere topped the Deere factories with large, copper-sculpted deer stags. The current trademark, with its stylized deer in silhouette, was introduced in mid-2000.

The Gilpin Sulky Plow, with leaping-deer insignia attached, and a two-bottom gang plow competed in the famous Paris Exhibition in 1878 at Petit-Bourg, France, and, according to Deere advertising, the plows were "victorious in all points." By 1883, Deere & Company sold more than 100,000 units overall, including moldboard plows, spring cultivators, harrows, and shovel plows. It is interesting to note that even with the success of the Gilpin Sulky Plow in the 1880s, Deere walking plows still outsold the plow with a seat by more than six to one.

Moore continued to improve the plow that carried his name. In 1881, a "power-lift" was added, which raised the plow as needed. The Gilpin Sulky Plow, with minor changes, continued to sell even after World War I.

Gilpin Moore is considered one of Deere & Company's most important product developers and inventors of the nineteenth century. When he retired in the 1890s, he held more than thirty-one patents in his name. He held another four patents jointly with other Deere employees.

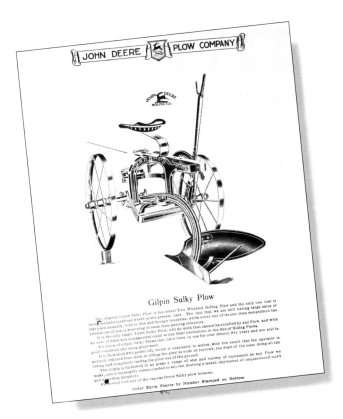

More sophisticated horse-drawn equipment followed the Gilpin Sulky Plow introduced in 1875. Deere inventor Gilpin Moore got it rolling and kept it going with improvements culminating in a power lift. (Deere & Company archives)

In 1876, the leaping deer sprang up as the primary Deere & Company trademark. (Deere & Company archives)

Corn planting became mechanized with early planters like this one made in Galesburg, Illinois. The seed "dropper" on the planter check-rowed the corn in time with marks previously scratched in the field across the direction of travel.

Sod attachments helped early Deere rotary-drop planters place seed in freshly turned sod. The Deere & Mansur planter effort was successful from its start in 1879. The company also made a less-expensive planter called the Moline.

A CORN PLANTER AT LAST

The typical prairie farmer's annual spring corn planting "when the oak leaves were as big as squirrel ears" was a short but intensive event for man, beast, and boy. The pattern of planting the crop in hills of four to six seeds had been set by eastern Native American tribes. In the spring of 1621, an English-speaking member of the Patuxet tribe named Squanto, or more formally Tisquantum, first showed the Pilgrim settlers how to plant Indian corn with a fish in each hill as starter fertilizer. By the 1850s, little had changed in the way corn was planted. Once the soil had been worked in the spring, it was marked into 42-inch (107-cm) squares (the approximate width of a horse) with a shovel-shaped plow, and four to six kernels of corn were dropped at the intersection of the furrows, then covered with dirt using a hoe. A fish in each hill wasn't necessary in the fertile prairie soils, but the job was still painfully slow.

Boys, usually saddled with the job of dropping corn, could plant only about an acre (0.4 ha) per day of the crudely check-rowed corn. "One for the cutworm, one for the crow, one for the squirrel, and three to grow!," sometimes recited as the corn was dropped in the hill, was a prophetic litany addressing plant population. With an average of only about twenty or so days of good weather each spring, time greatly limited the possible acreage that could be put to corn on a one-boy farm.

Early corn-planting devices were hand-held inventions capable of "dropping" a hill at a time. Two-hill versions of the hand dropper were made by connecting two of the one-hill droppers together.

A Galesburg, Illinois, factory made a popular two-row, rolling, horse-drawn wooden planter that was widely sold during and after the Civil War. Brown's Illinois Corn Planter had enclosed wooden wheels carrying the planter. They also served as seed press wheels as they ran on top of each row behind the wooden runners that opened a furrow for the seed. The seed dropper (another farm boy) rode between the seed boxes and operated a lever to drop the seeds in the two rows at each mark crossing the planter's direction of travel. Voilà! Check-row planting mechanized.

Aware of the success of the primitive two-row Brown planter and the growing need for fast and accurate planting, Charles Deere and Alvah Mansur formed a new and

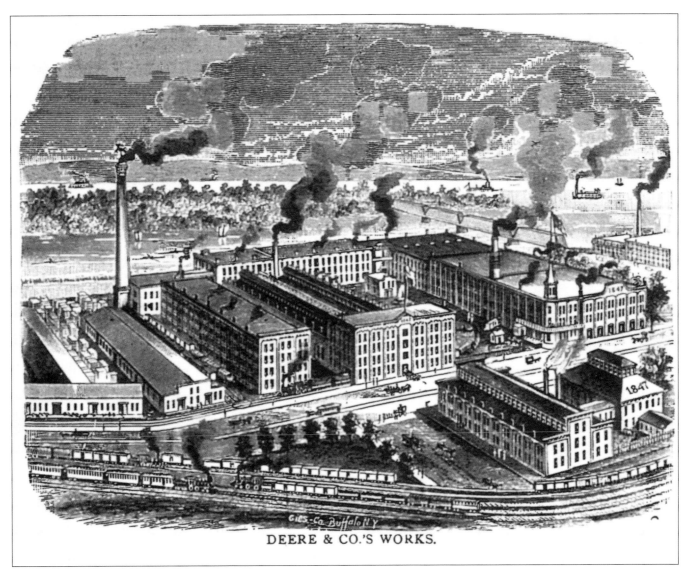

DEERE & CO.'S WORKS.

An 1890s-era view of Deere & Company's Moline works.

separate corporation in 1877 to build corn planters in Moline. Under the corporate name of Deere & Mansur Company they had their new "Deere Rotary Drop" planter ready by 1879. Although Brown's planter used a different drop mechanism than the Deere & Mansur machine, George Brown claimed a prior patent on the rotary drop mechanism, sued Deere & Mansur, and won. Whether Deere paid damages is not known, but the Deere & Mansur planter went on to become a popular machine after a check-rowing feature was added. Historian Broehl says Deere & Mansur made a $10,000 profit in 1879, and $48,000 by 1882. The separate Deere & Mansur Company didn't become a part of Deere & Company until 1909.

HALF A CENTURY WITH PLOWS

John Deere died May 17, 1886, at the age of eighty-two, almost fifty years after he first arrived on the Illinois prairie. Historians credit him with seeing value in new ideas and adapting them to his products to better serve his market and his customers. Rather than being a major inventor, Deere is considered an adapter of emerging technology and an imaginative marketer. His penchant for quality became a company tradition that saw the small one-man plow-making firm that he began with his muscles, forge, hammer, tongs, and anvil become the world's largest maker of farm implements.

Chapter 2

The Earliest Tractors

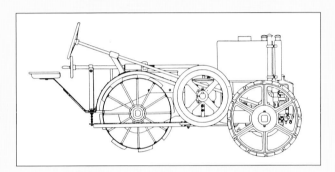

Above: *Line drawing of the proposed single-cylinder Sklovsky D-2 tractor, designed by John Deere engineer Max Sklovsky.*

Left: *A 1924 Waterloo Boy N owned by Jim Russell of Oblong, Illinois.*

J ohn Deere's first half-century saw the company start in a country village as a one-man operation, move on to an industrial location, and grow into its initial corporate shape. But during that period of growth and expansion, the company's product line stayed rather narrow, focused primarily on tilling the soil of the prairies.

Deere & Company, with its marketing efforts broadened and strengthened by its new branch houses, attacked the next quarter century with many additions to those early "earthy" tools. As the twentieth century got underway, Deere & Company made a careful investigation and study of farm equipment and its manufacturers, looking for lines that would complement its own strengths in tillage tools. The company then methodically added to its line almost all of the implements its customers used.

The Secretary single disk plow of the mid-1890s was the first John Deere disk plow. The Secretary was also made in double-disk versions.

THE MONSTER IN CHICAGO

Increased competition in the farm implement industry spurred Deere & Company's interest in strengthening and expanding their product line. In 1902, the International Harvester Company (IHC) of Chicago was formed, combining the assets of McCormick Harvesting Machine, Deering Harvester, Plano Manufacturing Company, Milwaukee Harvester Company, and Champion Harvester. In 1903, the D. M. Osborne Company was added to the IHC stable, and, in 1904, the Weber Wagon Company, Aultman-Miller, and the Keystone Company were folded into IHC, creating a huge company capable of dominating a large part of the farm equipment market with its diverse product line.

Over the previous years, Deere and McCormick Harvesting Machine Company avoided competing with each other by specializing in different lines of equipment. Deere & Company focused on plows and tillage tools, while McCormick concentrated its efforts on binders or "harvesters." However, that hands-off, mutually advantageous situation was soon to change after the formation of IHC.

DEERE BEEFS UP

Charles Deere died on October 29, 1907, in Chicago at the age of seventy. He had invested more than fifty years in managing the company his father started. Charles Deere's shoes would be hard to fill.

Elected to the president's post at the Deere board meeting November 26, 1907, was William Butterworth, husband of Katherine Deere, Charles Deere's daughter. Butterworth had served as company treasurer since 1894.

It didn't take long for Butterworth and the Deere directors to aggressively begin to build a collection of firms to create a more diverse Deere & Company. Between 1907 and 1912, Butterworth and the Deere board of directors added the Fort Smith Wagon Company; formed John Deere Plow Company Ltd. in Canada; organized the John Deere Export Company in New York City; and bought the Marseilles Manufacturing Company of Marseilles, Illinois, for their line of corn shellers and elevators. Deere also acquired Kemp & Burpee of Syracuse, New York, for manure spreaders; took over the Dain Manufacturing Company of Ottumwa, Iowa, and Welland, Ontario, to add haymaking tools to the line; brought the Deere & Mansur corn planters and its other tools into the Deere & Company fold; added the Syracuse Chilled Plow Company; brought in Union Malleable Iron of Moline and the Reliance Buggy Company of St. Louis; bought Van Brunt of Horicon, Wisconsin, for grain drills; and put the John Deere Wagon Works under Deere & Company.

Deere & Company also diversified its line by internal initiatives. Since it had not acquired a harvester by purchase or merger, Deere decided to design and build its own grain binder, a move which would put the company in head-to-head competition with IHC. The John Deere binder was designed in the winter of 1909–1910 by a former McCormick-Deering employee, Harry J. Podlesak. That spring A. C. Funk, former superintendent of the IHC Champion Works, came to Moline to head the Deere harvester department. Construction on the company's new Harvester Works plant began in the summer of 1912 and was in full operation by 1914, turning out 12,000 binders in the first year of production.

Through these changes, Deere & Company was beefing up to compete with the monster in Chicago—the IHC company.

William Butterworth, son-in-law of Charles Deere, was Deere & Company president from 1907 until 1928. His presidency saw the company add many companies and products from 1907 through 1912. (Deere & Company archives)

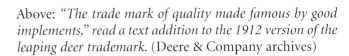

Above: *"The trade mark of quality made famous by good implements,"* read a text addition to the 1912 version of the leaping deer trademark. (Deere & Company archives)

Left: *Plows and other tillage tools were Deere & Company's primary products until it brought other companies and their products under its corporate umbrella starting in 1907. This two-bottom sulky gang plow was photographed in spring 1963 on an Amish farm on the Illinois prairies near Arthur. A spike-toothed harrow dragged behind the plow conserved soil moisture.*

International Harvester finally replied in 1919 to Deere's move into binders when it bought the Parlin & Orendorff Company of Canton, Illinois, the third-ranked plow maker in the United States. Without a doubt, Deere & Company now had serious competition in plows.

Deere & Company had assembled some of the best farm tools and their makers to become a major full-line agricultural implement manufacturer. Its new competitive stance put it nearly head to head with the mammoth IHC. But it had yet to approach the hot topic of gasoline traction engines. IHC, by contrast, had tractors on the market as early as 1905.

A "tractor plow" with undermounted three-bottom plow was Deere & Company's first attempt at developing its own tractor. This three-wheeler was designed by C. H. Melvin in 1912. Only one was built, and work on it stopped in 1914. (Deere & Company archives)

Deere had stayed out of the manufacture of steam engines and threshing machines during their boom years in the late 1880s, and Deere was apparently still reluctant to add tractors to its product line as the 1900s opened. Deere management could see many firms in financial trouble because of the behemoth tractors those firms were trying to sell when the market suddenly shifted to smaller tractors. Deere decided to wait until the market settled.

Although in 1910 the St. Louis and Atlanta Deere branch houses sold the Big Four 30 gasoline tractor made by the Gas Traction Company of Minneapolis, and Deere & Company listed the Twin City Model 40 tractor for export sales to South America in 1912, Deere & Company itself seemed content to just supply tractor-drawn gang plows to other firms that were making and selling tractors.

THE FIRST DEERE TRACTOR DESIGNS

The future pulled up alongside Deere and threatened to pass it by as the two major implement companies girded to do competitive battle. Deere's own branch houses and dealers began to pressure the company to make a tractor, and in March 1912, Deere authorized C. H. Melvin, a Deere engineer from the experimental department, to develop a "tractor plow." One such tractor was built in 1912, a three-wheeler similar to a model called the Hackney Motor Plow built in St. Paul, Minnesota. The prototype Deere tractor had an undermounted three-bottom plow and could be configured to work either forward or backward, with the two drive wheels going first, or with the single wheel going first like a tricycle.

However, work on the tractor plow was stopped in 1914. In May, Joseph Dain, Sr., who had become a vice

Walter Silver, Plow Works experimental engineer, devised this two-row John Deere motor cultivator in 1916–17. It was propelled by its front wheels and steered on row end turns with the small rear wheel. This No. 4 model used foot controls to help it dodge quickly through ragged check-rowed corn. (Deere & Company archives)

Motor Cultivators

Other early Deere tractor efforts were aimed at a concept popular among manufacturers between 1915 and 1920: the "motor cultivator." The motor cultivator was designed just for cultivating row crops, which was still carried out by teams of horses on most farms. Farm equipment marketing people relished a specialized machine that might prompt the farmer to buy two tractors instead of one. They hoped he would need a primary tractor for tillage and a horse-replacing motor cultivator to control the weeds in his corn.

In 1916–1917, Joseph Dain, Sr., and Theo Brown, head of Deere's experimental division, developed a prototype one-row motor cultivator with a 7½-hp New Way air-cooled engine. Brown, a 1901 Worcester Polytechnic Institute graduate in mechanical engineering, had been named head of the experimental department at the John Deere Plow Works in 1916 and was named Deere & Company chief engineer in 1923. The motor cultivator design featured a two-wheeled one-row cultivator with a rear-mounted power unit running on manure-spreader wheels. An articulated steering arrangement let the operator turn at row ends with a steering wheel that pivoted the machine in the center. Row dodging and steering the cultivator down the row was done with the cultivator's foot pedals.

The one-row machine was redesigned with a larger two-cylinder hopper-cooled engine designed by McVicker of Minneapolis and built by Associated Manufacturers of Waterloo, Iowa. Twenty-five of these four-wheeled "Tractivators" were built in 1917 and sent out that spring for testing, but the test results were disappointing. It still didn't have enough power, and the hopper cooling had to be refilled often. The tests concluded that the Tractivator really did no more work than a good team of horses. However, the engineers had proven to themselves that corn could be properly cultivated with a motor cultivator. They had also converted the little machine into a capable small tractor by running it with the drive wheels forward and mounting implements on or behind the cultivator wheels.

But despite these successes, work on the Tractivator soon ground to a halt. When rival IHC introduced its two-row motor cultivator in 1917, Deere designers quit work on their one-row unit and developed their own two-row machine.

A later John Deere two-row design, built of available parts in two weeks time, was the company's first three-wheeled motor cultivator. Designed by Walter Silver, an engineer in and later the manager of the Plow Works Experimental Department, the cultivator had two large drive wheels in front and was steered with a small rear wheel. Silver's prototype machine had an Avery engine equipped with friction drive centered over the two front drive wheels. Field trials in June 1917 revealed problems with steering precision, and the machine was redesigned and improved. Silver's No. 3 and No. 4 Motor Cultivators provided steering control of the wide-spaced front drive wheels through foot controls, enabling the operator to steer quickly to track the two rows being cultivated. Turning around at the end of the rows was still accomplished by steering with the single rear wheel.

Although tests of five of the two-row machines as cultivators and general purpose tractors were promising, the motor cultivator seemed a concept whose time had passed. Lack of power to work two rows pushed the design back to a one-row concept by 1921, and the post–World War I recession along with tight engineering budgets closed down the project that same year.

All three wheels helped pull the next John Deere tractor. That tractor, the All-Wheel-Drive, was developed between 1916 and 1917 by Joe Dain, whose Dain Manufacturing Company of Ottumwa, Iowa, had been purchased by Deere. (Deere & Company archives)

president at Deere in 1910 when it acquired his Ottumwa, Iowa, hay equipment company, was authorized by the Deere board of directors to develop a new tractor design for the company.

THE DEERE ALL-WHEEL-DRIVE TRACTOR

To meet the price competition of the day, Deere assigned a target price of $700 for its new tractor. Dain's design approach was also for a three-wheeler (then a popular concept), but the machine he designed had all three of its wheels pulling. It was initially powered by a four-cylinder, vertical, inline Waukesha engine. The first John Deere prototype All-Wheel-Drive tractor was built in 1915, tested, improved, and re-tested.

More test units were built and field tested in 1916 and 1917. In September 1917, Deere decided to build a trial production run of 100 All-Wheel-Drive tractors.

In its final form the Deere All-Wheel-Drive machine was powered with a four-cylinder, McVicker-designed 4½x6-inch (114x152-mm) bore-and-stroke engine delivering a rated 12 drawbar and 24 belt hp. It weighed about 4,600 pounds (726 kg) and was expected to be sold as a two-to-three-plow tractor. Advanced design features included a new shift-on-the-go transmission with two speeds of 2 and 2⅝ mph (3.2 and 4.3 km/h) both forward

and backward. The three-wheeler featured two wheels in front and one wide wheel in the rear. The front wheels were 36 inches (91 cm) in diameter and 8 inches (20 cm) wide. The rear wheel was larger and wider, measuring 40 inches (102 cm) in diameter and 20 inches (51 cm) wide. The front wheels turned left and right to steer the tractor. The All-Wheel-Drive tractor was built in Deere's Tenth Street factory in East Moline, Illinois, and all 100 were completed during 1919. There are only two known examples of the interesting John Deere All-Wheel-Drive tractors in running condition today.

Joseph Dain died suddenly in November 1917, before the new tractor was built. On March 14, 1918, before production of the All-Wheel-Drives tractors was complete, Deere & Company bought the Waterloo Gasoline Engine Company of Waterloo, Iowa, manufacturers of the famous Waterloo Boy tractors and stationary engines. Although all 100 Deere All-Wheel-Drive tractors were manufactured and sold, the Waterloo Boy purchase, and probably Joseph Dain's death, doomed the All-Wheel-Drive design. In addition, the price of the All-Wheel-Drive machine had risen to $1,700 compared with only $985 for the Waterloo Boy, an amount much closer to Deere's target price of $700 to enter the tractor market.

Tough plowing conditions breaking out sod and brush showed the superior traction of the three driving wheels of the John Deere All-Wheel-Drive tractor. One hundred tractors were made and sold before it was scrapped in favor of a simpler design—the Waterloo Boy. (Deere & Company archives)

A LIGHT TWO-PLOW TRACTOR

Around the same time Deere was at work on the All-Wheel-Drive tractor, the company was also designing a lightweight two-plow tractor. In charge of that project was Max Sklovsky, Deere's chief engineer.

Max Sklovsky was the first engineering school graduate at Deere & Company. He joined the firm in 1902 as a technical engineer with a degree in electrical engineering from Armour Institute of Technology (now the Illinois Institute of Technology) in Chicago. Max became Deere chief engineer in 1911 after earning a master's degree in mechanical engineering from Armour.

Like the All-Wheel-Drive tractor, the Sklovsky project was a four-cylinder, three-wheel design. Other elements of the design were unique, with a one-piece, cast-iron body extending from the engine crankcase back to the rear wheel. A Northway four-cylinder gas engine powered the tractor, and prototypes were built as Models A-2 and B-2. Automotive-type steering on the B-2 version improved on the pivoting single axle of the Model A-2. The tractor was designed to sell for about $900. One objection to the design was that the Northway engine didn't burn kerosene, the low-cost fuel of the day then considered an important attribute for a farm tractor.

Under market pressures, the Sklovsky model continued to evolve. A third prototype, the D-2 was a smaller machine with a single-cylinder engine, a design aimed at bringing the tractor's price down to about $600. But development of the lightweight tractor was ended at the advent of World War I by the appearance of the popular, low-priced Fordson tractor.

Though Sklovsky's tractor never made it into production, the engineer himself enjoyed a long career with the company. He went on to design and install many manufacturing facilities and improvements as the company grew. He earned twenty-six patents before his retirement in 1944 after forty-two years at Deere & Company.

Deere's internal efforts to break into the tractor market came to a grinding halt and then completely switched gears in 1918, when the company acquired the Waterloo Gasoline Engine Company, including that company's line of Waterloo Boy tractors.

A light two-plow tractor with all-wheel drive was built by Deere & Company in 1915–1916. This three-wheel design by Max Sklovsky, the company's chief engineer, had a four-cylinder inline Northway engine. Its single-unit cast construction was unique. This B-2 model steered with automotive-type steering. Designer Sklovsky is shown in the driver's seat. (Deere & Company archives)

JOHN FROELICH.

Iowan John Froelich made one of the world's first gasoline tractors in 1892.

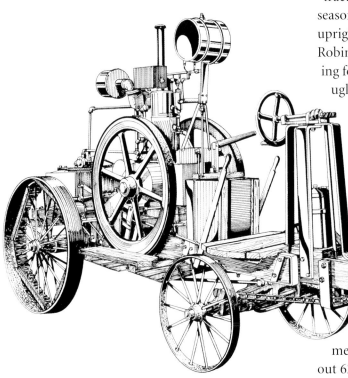

In 1892, before anything like it was available, custom thresherman John Froelich built this tractor to power his J. I. Case threshing machine. The Waterloo Gasoline Traction Engine Company, which he and others set up in 1893, later became the Waterloo Gas Engine Company, maker of the Waterloo Boy tractor. (Deere & Company archives)

JOHN FROELICH'S TRACTOR

John Froelich was forty-three in 1892 when he began talking about the future of internal-combustion mechanical power and its use on operations as small as medium-sized farms. Some of his neighbors mused John might have been out in the sun too long, but they kept their cynicism quiet because they had seen him in operation before: Froelich could make things happen. At the time, Froelich was running a grain elevator in Froelich, Iowa (a village named for his father), digging wells thereabouts, and doing custom threshing in Iowa and South Dakota each summer and fall with a straw-burning steam engine belted to his threshing machine. There was little else but straw close at hand to burn in those far-off fields, but Froelich was looking for a source of energy easier to carry and stoke than straw. He already knew about steam farm power and how to harness it, but he wanted something better. Gasoline looked like it might be the answer.

In 1892, Froelich assembled a crude-looking gasoline "tractor" that he used successfully in that year's threshing season in Iowa and South Dakota. Froelich mounted an upright Van Duzen single-cylinder gasoline engine on a Robinson engine chassis and then devised his own gearing for propulsion of the machine. His hybrid worked—ugly as it was.

The Van Duzen engine on Froelich's machine was rated at 20 hp from its one 14x14-inch (356x356-mm) bore-and-stroke, vertical "jug" and piston. Electric ignition from a battery and coil through breaker points fired the charged cylinder. A flyball governor opened the exhaust valve and closed the intake valve to allow it to coast down when the engine was above speed.

Not only could the Froelich gasoline traction engine go forward and backward under its own power, but once belted to Froelich's J. I. Case 40x58-inch (102x147-cm) threshing machine, it powered his thresher for the 1892 summer and fall fifty-two-day harvest season and threshed out 62,000 bushels (2.2 million liters) of grain. That was a notable achievement for a self-propelled, internal-combustion engine in that era when steam power was king. Many historians consider the Froelich machine the first practical tractor. It presaged convenient lightweight gasoline power for farm work and set the stage for Froelich to found a company to build the tractors.

THE WATERLOO BOY

The Waterloo Gasoline Traction Engine Company, the eventual builder of the Waterloo Boy Tractor, was organized in 1893 by John Froelich and others. The company built four more tractors in 1893, but only two were sold,

Stationary gasoline or kerosene engines ranging from 2 to 25 hp were the main products of the Waterloo Gasoline Engine Company early on. Tractors began to show up in company ads starting about 1914.

both of which were returned for inadequacies. Although another tractor was built in 1896 and yet another in 1897, the young company decided to concentrate on stationary gasoline engines instead of tractors. Froelich's primary interest was in the gas tractor, and he dropped out of the firm in 1895 when it was reorganized as the Waterloo Gasoline Engine Company.

By 1906, the company had named its twelve sizes of portable and stationary engines of 1½ to 22 hp "Waterloo Boys." By 1912, the H series of stationary engines in sizes from 2 to 14 hp were in production.

In 1911, renewed interest in the potential market for tractors after the success of other gas tractors led the Waterloo, Iowa, company to again work on tractor designs. By 1912, a vertical four-cylinder cross-mounted four-cycle engine of 25 hp powered a big tractor they called the Waterloo Boy Standard. In 1914, the company designed and

built twenty-nine Waterloo Boy Model L and LA tractors, which were 15-hp two-cylinder horizontally opposed models. Nine of them had three wheels, and the other twenty were four-wheeled versions.

THE WATERLOO BOY BECOMES THE "GRANDPOPPA"

By 1914, an early version of the Waterloo Boy Model R was built with an integral block for its two cylinders. This design succeeded and is considered the "Grandpoppa" of the John Deere line. Its twin horizontal cylinder heads faced to the rear near the operator platform. Its side-by-side engine with a 180-degree-opposed crankshaft throw, set the pattern and the familiar "pop-pop-pause" exhaust rhythm for later John Deere engines. The R had one speed of 2½ mph (4 km/h) either forward or in reverse.

When Deere & Company bought the Waterloo Gaso-

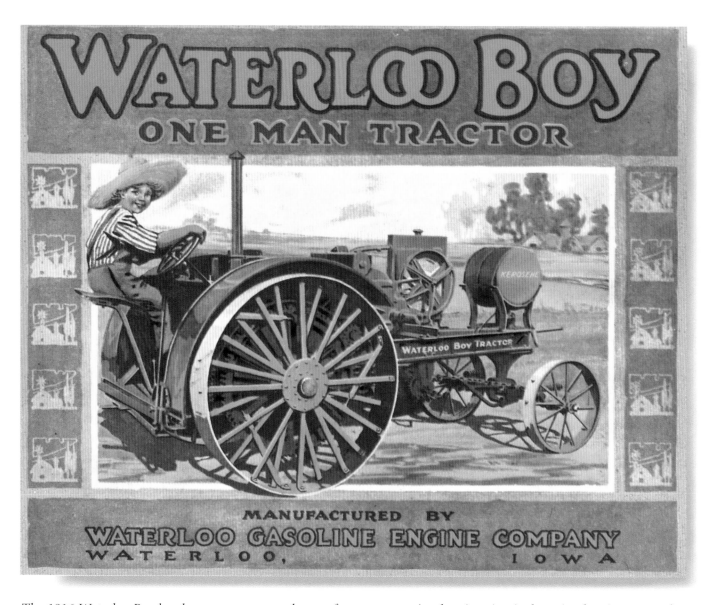

The 1916 Waterloo Boy brochure cover suggested ease of tractor operation by picturing its beaming boy in a straw hat driving the Model R.

line Engine Company in 1918, the later Model N was kept in production. The N included a two-speed transmission with forward speeds of 2¼ and 3 mph (3.6 and 4.8 km/h) and 2¼ mph (3.6 km/h) in reverse. John Deere soon stiffened the frame of the N by replacing bolts with rivets. Roller chains replaced link chains on the tractor's final drive to solve another weakness in design.

DEERE BUYS THE WATERLOO GASOLINE ENGINE COMPANY

In early 1918, after Deere & Company's halting steps to develop its own tractor nearly bogged down, the company authorized board member Frank Silloway to investigate a report that the Waterloo Gasoline Engine Company was for sale. Silloway, then in charge of Deere sales, made the contact, investigated the company, and enthusiastically reported back to the board recommending that Deere & Company purchase the Iowa firm.

If acquired, the Waterloo factory with its sturdy, uncomplicated, practical tractor, could put Deere & Company into first place in the tractor business overnight, Silloway argued. There had been 4,558 Waterloo Boy tractors made in 1917, he told the board, up from 2,762 in 1916. That 1917 figure later proved to be overstated, but it didn't change the unfolding events.

The board stood unanimously behind Silloway and approved his motion to buy the tractor company. In March 1918, for $2,350,000, Deere & Company bought the Waterloo Gasoline Engine Company and was suddenly in the tractor business—with both feet.

THE MODEL N AND THE FIRST NEBRASKA TRACTOR TEST

In 1920, when the University of Nebraska at Lincoln initiated its now well-known tractor tests, the Waterloo Boy Model N was the first tractor tested. The University of Nebraska developed standardized tests for tractor performance after the state passed a law requiring tractors sold in Nebraska be tested for performance. The law was designed to protect tractor buyers from misleading claims by manufacturers. The Nebraska tests soon became a standard in the United States, and most tractors made or sold in the country since 1920 have been Nebraska-tested.

Belt horsepower was measured at Nebraska by belting the tractor to a dynamometer in a static test that measured power output from each tractor's belt pulley. Drawbar horsepower was measured with the tractor in motion pulling a test "car" equipped with instruments reading power pulled by its drawbar. Test conditions were standardized so tractor ratings could be compared one with another. A less accurate but commonly used informal rating of tractor power for comparing machines was how many 14-inch (36-cm) plow bottoms a tractor could pull under average conditions. After tractor power takeoffs (PTOs) virtually replaced the use of belt pulleys on tractors, the Nebraska tests used output measurements taken from the PTO. The 1959 John Deere Model 435 diesel was the first tractor Nebraska-tested for a PTO horsepower rating.

The 6,183-pound (2,807-kg) Waterloo Boy Model N, advertised as "The Original Kerosene Tractor," rated 12.1 drawbar and 25.51 belt hp in the pioneering Nebraska tests. Its kerosene-burning engine was a 6½x7-inch (165x178-mm) bore-and-stroke operating at 750 rpm. Heat from the tractor's exhaust manifold was used to help vaporize the kerosene for complete combustion in the cylinders. The tractor was rated as a three-plow tractor, meaning it could pull three 14-inch (36-cm) plow bottoms under most field conditions.

In 1920, Deere added automotive-type front-wheel steering to the Waterloo Boy N, replacing the earlier fixed axle with its chain-wrap steering. Improved versions of the Model N continued in production until 1924 when it was replaced with the John Deere Model D.

CATCH UP TIME

Deere came late to the tractor business and was intent to catch up. Competition, especially from the Fordson and the new IHC 15/30 and 10/20 "gear drive" tractors, was pushing the firm to action. Sales of Henry Ford's lightweight 2,700-pound (1,226-kg) tractor, in particular,

were soaring. During the time Deere was getting on line with the Waterloo Boy in 1918–1920, Ford sold 158,000 Fordsons. By comparison, only about 13,700 Waterloo Boys were sold in the same period. The Fordson sales continued strong, and, in 1923, after a price cut to only $395, Fordson sales accounted for 76 percent of all gas tractors sold in the United States that year.

Times were tight at Deere during the economic recession after World War I, but if the firm was going to stay in the tractor business, it needed to replace the dated Waterloo Boy with an improved machine. Would it be a four-cylinder tractor as were Deere's earliest designs? Economics of manufacture, maintenance, and operation prevailed: Deere stayed with the tested Waterloo Boy concept and produced only two-cylinder tractors for the next forty years.

John Deere bought the Waterloo Gasoline Engine Company in 1918 and added the Waterloo Boy kerosene tractor to the John Deere line. John Deere made and sold the Model N Waterloo Boy from 1918 until it was replaced by the new John Deere D in 1924. The Waterloo Boy was never badged with the John Deere name.

Kerosene was gravity fed from the front-mounted fuel tank to the engine in the rear. A side-mounted fan-blown radiator cooled the engine.

Above: *A removeable crank helped start the Waterloo Boy's two-cylinder engine.*

Left: *John Deere improvements to the Waterloo Boy were a riveted frame, steel roller chains in the final drive, and automotive-type steering. This 1924 Waterloo Boy N has the John Deere changes. Original Waterloo Boys had chain-wrap steering moving their wagon-type axles for steering. Three-plow power and cheap fuel helped make the Waterloo Boy popular. It proved its power in the first-ever University of Nebraska tractor performance test with a demonstrated 12.1 drawbar hp and 25.51 belt hp. Illinois collector Jim Russell has replaced the tractor's cleats with rubber belting for a better ride on pavement during parades.*

CHAPTER 3

From the D to the L:
John Deere's First Tractors

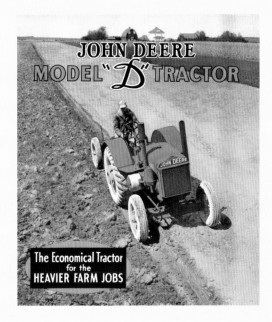

Above: *The unmuffled, two-cylinder John Deere Model D, with its staccato report, soon earned the nickname "Johnny Popper." Neighbors a mile away could tell field conditions by how loudly Johnny popped.*

Left: *An early 1928 Model GP owned by Don and Marty Huber of Moline, Illinois.*

Deere & Company entered its Power Farming era in 1918 with the purchase of the company that made the Waterloo Boy tractor. The "new" tractor enjoyed good sales for a couple of years, but sales of the Waterloo Boy Model N plunged to only 79 tractors in 1921 from 5,045 units in 1920 as a sour economy and tough competition took its toll. In early 1922, Henry Ford dropped the price of his Fordson tractor to only $395 compared with an already reduced $890 for the Waterloo Boy. IHC responded to Ford's move by dropping prices by $230 each on two of its McCormick-Deering models.

The heat was on. Fortunately, John Deere engineers were working on a new design and, by 1921, were well underway to evolving the stodgy Waterloo Boy into the Model D that became the founding father of a long two-cylinder tractor dynasty.

THE D

The "Poppa" of all Deere two-cylinder tractors was developed in Waterloo, Iowa, from ideas first used in the "Grandpoppa"—the Waterloo Boy tractor.

Between 1919 and 1922, John Deere built and tested experimental versions of a new tractor roughly based on the Waterloo Boy at the John Deere Waterloo Tractor Works. Designs and prototypes were developed in four styles designated as A, B, C, and D. The last of those styles, the Model D John Deere 15/27 tractor of 1923, was the design that made it to market, the first of the Waterloo two-cylinder tractors to carry the John Deere name. The engine in the D was mounted with its two cylinders facing forward instead of backward, as on the Waterloo Boy. The engine crankshaft carried a hefty open-spoked 26-inch (66-cm) diameter flywheel on the left and a belt pulley with an internal clutch on the right. The tractor was started by opening cylinder petcocks to reduce the compression, pulling the flywheel by hand through compression on a power stroke, then closing the petcocks on engine start—a starting procedure that soon became common on John Deere tractors. Those first Model Ds with the spoked flywheel are today called "Spokers" by lovers of the genre.

The D was a three-plow, standard-tread tractor with an all-enclosed drive train, pressure lubrication, and thermo-syphon cooling. Like its predecessor, the D was designed to run on kerosene or distillates. It produced 22 drawbar and 30 belt hp when first tested at Nebraska in 1924. Its two-cylinder 6½x7-inch (165x178-mm) bore-and-stroke engine turned at 800 rpm. The two-speed transmission moved it forward at 2½ and 3¼ mph (3.2 and 5.2 km/h) and backward at 2 mph (3.2 km/h). Operating weight was about 4,000 pounds (1,816 kg), or about

All-enclosed final drive and frameless construction made the Model D a "light, powerful, simple" farm tractor, Deere ads claimed. This 1925 "Spoker" D has the 24-inch (61-cm) spoked flywheel that replaced the 26-inch (66-cm) spoked flywheel used on the first Ds. A solid flywheel was used starting in 1926. The first Ds were tested at 22 drawbar and 30 belt hp. Ken and Bob Burden of New London, Iowa, restored this classic. By 1928 it was a more powerful tractor with a 28.53/36.98 horsepower test made possible by adding ¼ inch (6.5 mm) to the cylinder bore to bring it to 6¾ inches (171 mm).

The John Deere Model D became the "Poppa" of all John Deere tractors. It set the pattern for all the two-cylinder tractors that followed. This 1928 D, owned by West Liberty, Ohio, collector Richard Kimball, has yellow trim on the flywheel rim. He says a 1939 family movie of the tractor at work shows the extra color. John Deere purists find no evidence the D flywheel ever carried that stripe of color and figure it was added after the tractor left the factory.

2,100 pounds (953 kg) less than the Waterloo Boy it replaced. Water injected into the cylinders when the tractor was under heavy load helped the D burn distillate fuels without power-robbing pre-ignition or knocking.

Rear steel drive wheels were 46x12 inches (117x30 cm) wide with 28x5-inch (71x13-cm) steel wheels on the front, compared with the Waterloo Boy's 52x12-inch (132x30-cm) rear and 28x6-inch (71x13-cm) front wheels. The Deere engineers designed the D as a more compact tractor, too. It was about 23 inches (58 cm) shorter, 9 inches (23 cm) narrower, and 7 inches (18 cm) lower than the Waterloo Boy. Gone was the steel frame that carried the separate, spread-out components of its ancestors. The D was of integral frame construction with the transmission case and engine castings bolted together carrying their own load.

The first fifty John Deere Ds had a fabricated front axle assembly that was replaced later with a one-piece cast unit. Those early tractors also had a distinguishing ladder-look to the sides of their radiators. Originally, the driver steered the tractor from a left-hand seat, but, in 1931, the driver's seat was moved to the right side.

The flywheel was downsized to a 24-inch (61-cm) diameter spoked design in 1924 and 1925 after 879 tractors with the 26-inch (66-cm) flywheel were made from 1923 to 1924. Another 4,876 Ds with the spoked 24-inch (61-cm) flywheel were made in 1924 and 1925. Beginning in 1926, the flywheel became a solid casting but retained the key and keyway attachment to the crankshaft of the earlier open-spoked models. In 1927 and later, flywheels were attached by way of splines in the crankshaft end mated with matching grooves inside the flywheel.

Advertisements for the Model D made the case for the machine's "Few and sturdier parts—made over-size—of the finest materials and workmanship. Complete enclosure of working parts in a dust-proof, oil-tight case, thoroughly lubricated by a simple, positive oiling system. Most efficient final drive ever designed for tractors," the ad continued, "Double roller chains of hardened steel, completely enclosed and running in oil bath." The ad concluded, "Low initial cost, fuel and oil economy, faster working speeds, low upkeep cost and long life make it a safe, money-making investment for the future." Deere also noted in its ads that the tractor had a "straight line transmission with no bevel gears to consume power."

To show the inherent smooth operation of their two-cylinder engine, Deere demonstrators balanced the Model D on four pop bottles in displays at the Illinois and Iowa State Fairs in 1929. Thus suspended, the D chugged away with the transmission in gear and the drive wheels turning, showing there wasn't enough rhythmic vibration from the chugging two-cylinder engine to topple the running tractor from its precarious perch on the narrow-topped bottles.

Addition of ¼ inch (6.5 mm) to the cylinder bore and an improved carburetor in 1928 boosted horsepower of the D to 28 drawbar and 36 belt. The tractor got a boost in rpm in 1931 from 800 up to 900. In 1935, a three-speed transmission was added. By the end of its long production run in 1953, power of the D had been moved up to 38 hp on the drawbar and 42 on the belt.

The D was produced continuously for thirty years, the longest production run of one model ever. Some 160,000 Model Ds were made from 1924 to its end of production in the summer of 1953. Interestingly, the final ninety-two units were assembled outside the factory that summer on company streets and are today referred to as "Streeters" by Deere aficionados.

The John Deere Model D set the pattern for the entire family of rugged two-cylinder tractors Deere produced over the next thirty-five years. The tractor family all used the two-cylinder, forward-facing engine started by turning a massive left-side flywheel. And no bevel gears were used in any of their tractors until the vertical inline engine began to be used in Deere's smaller utility tractors.

After it's release in 1924, the D and later generations of Deere two-cylinder tractors took on a nickname: "Johnny Popper." Nicknamed for the distinctive two-cylinder unmuffled exhaust note, the name stuck, and even today John Deere two-cylinder tractors are called "Johnny Poppers," or "Popping Johnnies."

The D's pan seat was suspended over the drawbar with gear shift and hand clutch in front and to the right.

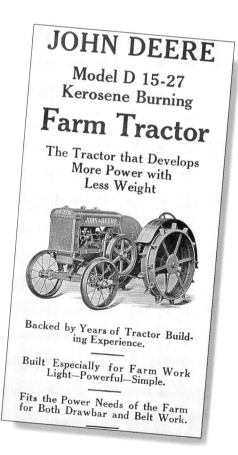

A 1924 Model D brochure.

Thermo-syphon circulation through the fan-blown radiator cooled the D. Water from the cooling system was injected into the cylinders to reduce knocking caused by pre-ignition when the engine was under heavy loads.

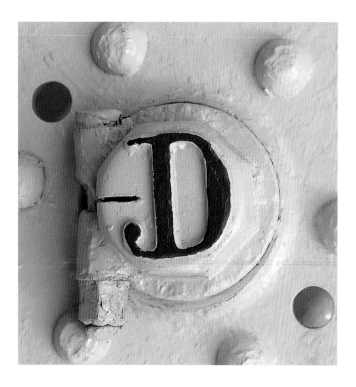

D wheel hub with John Deere monogram.

THE ROW-CROP CHALLENGE

With the arrival and early success of International Harvester Company's two-row, row-crop, tricycle-configured Farmall in 1924, Deere could not ignore the need for a row-crop or General Purpose tractor—one machine that could handle traditional tillage as well as row-crop cultivation. The Farmall was already ransacking the popular Fordson's sales with their versatile tricycle row-crop machine that could handle more farm jobs than the Fordson. It soon became evident to Deere & Company's marketing people that a tractor designed from the ground up to cultivate row crops, as well as to pull tillage tools and run belt applications, was a competitive necessity.

Deere began work on its All-Crop three-row cultivating tractor in 1926 under Theo Brown's leadership. After two years of prototype testing, production started on the new tractor in 1927. It was originally designated the Model C, and twenty-four were built. Another seventy-five Cs were added later that year.

The possible confusion between the spoken "dee" and "cee" is said to have caused reconsideration of the model designation, and, in 1928, the new tractor became the GP, the initials for General Purpose. Part numbers cast in the GP parts retained their C prefix during the production life of the tractor. Of the ninety-nine initial Model Cs, fifty-three are known to have received new serial numbers when they were recalled to the factory, redesignated Model GPs, rebuilt to improve on defects, and sent back to the fields. Some Cs apparently escaped the new GP designation and renumbering, and only one is known to survive.

Despite some early work on tricycle-type two-row machines during the time the C was in prototype stage, the GP was introduced in 1928 as a standard four-wheel configuration designed to handle three crop rows. An arched front axle and drop-gear housings to the rear axles gave it crop clearance to cultivate three rows. The tractor straddled the center row with the front wheels and the drive wheels centered between each outside row. It resembled the Model D in many respects but was smaller and had more clearance under the chassis and the arched front end. Its two-cylinder, kerosene-burning engine gave the GP a rated 10 drawbar and 20 belt hp from its 5¾x6-inch (146x152-mm) bore-and-stroke engine revolving at 950 rpm. Water injection under load helped minimize pre-ignition power loss. It was considered a two-plow tractor.

The GP had a three-speed transmission giving it speeds of 2¼, 3, and 4 mph (3.6, 4.8, and 6.4 km/h) forward and 1¾ mph (2.8 km/h) in reverse. It rolled on 24x6-inch (61x15-cm) steel wheels in front and 42¾x10-inch (109x25-cm) rear drive wheels. Its weight of 3,600 pounds (1,634 kg) was about a quarter ton (227 kg) less than the larger D.

The GP carried forward the same hands-on-flywheel starting as the D. Compression release valves on the two cylinders helped reduce the grip-and-grunt needed to get the engine firing. James and Terry Thompson of Laurelville, Ohio, restored this 1928 John Deere GP three-row tractor.

John Deere advertised it as "The Two-Plow Tractor that Plants and Cultivates Three Rows At A Time. . . . One man with his General Purpose does as much as two to four men using horses. . . . With four forms of power—drawbar, belt, power take-off plus a power lift—there are few farm jobs on which it cannot be profitably used."

The GP introduced a motor-driven power lift for its mounted three-row cultivator and planter. For the first time, "Power Farming" had started to include the comfort and convenience of the operator in addition to the tractor's power or pull in the field. The GP provided four sources of power to its user. Drawbar power for pulling implements; belt pulley power for running non-attached belt-driven machines such as grinders, shellers, etc.; power takeoff (PTO) to run tractor-mounted machines such as mowers and other attachments needing tractor power; and an integral mechanical power lift to raise and lower

attached implements. The power lift was an industry first for John Deere; competing tractor makers soon added power lifts to their tractor designs.

Despite all of this, the GP was an early disappointment to some row-crop owners—and even to John Deere management. Not all farmers were thrilled with the three-row concept, particularly cotton growers who were accustomed to two- and four-row planters and cultivators. Some row-crop farmers had trouble seeing the center or "straddle" row when cultivating. In addition, a lack of power to handle the three-row cultivator under some conditions was noted. The power problem was addressed in 1931 with an increase in the cylinder bore by ¼ inch (6.5 mm) up to 6 inches (152 mm). That boost in horsepower moved it from its original 10/20 horsepower rating up to 15/24. With the advent of the larger bore engine, water injection was dropped.

Above: *Power lifting of mounted implements was an industry first on the Model C and GP John Deere tractors. This gear box and revolving shaft with lever arm transmitted engine power to raise and lower implements.*

Left: *Row-crop clearance on the three-row GP was accomplished by an arched front axle and gear boxes on the rear axles to boost the tractor above the straddled row. The GP left the Waterloo, Iowa, factory in August 1928, following the earlier production there of ninety-nine Model C John Deere tractors. Fifty-three of the C models were reworked and given new GP serial numbers.*

GP magneto.

Wheel scraper on GP rear wheel.

Center planter seed box in operator platform on Bourgeois's GP.

"The two-plow tractor of standard design that plants and cultivates three rows at a time," John Deere advertising claimed for the GP. This 1931 model with its three-row mounted planter was restored by Wayne Bourgeois of Kahoka, Missouri. Old rubber tractor treads have been attached to the steel rims to make the tractor parade friendly.

Above: *Traditional John Deere flywheel starting was preserved on the GPO by letting part of the flywheel project from the orchard shielding of the left rear wheel.*

Left: *An orchard version of the GP, the GPO, was made from 1931 to the end of production of the model in 1935. A lowered profile with orchard fenders gave the tractor its distinctive look. Wayne Bourgeois of Kahoka, Missouri, restored this GPO.*

TRICYCLE TOO

The GP design was broadened at the end of the twenties, as Deere produced a tricycle two-row version of the machine. Seventy were built as tricycle GPs in 1928 and 1929. Only two of them are known to exist today. In 1929, up to six tricycle GPs with 68-inch (173-cm) rear wheel tread were made, a tread width later used on the potato version of the GP, allowing the tractor to straddle two 34-inch (86-cm) rows. But for a two- or four-row cultivator for corn, the tractor needed a rear tread width of 84 inches (213 cm) to straddle two 42-inch (107-cm) rows.

By the corn cropping season of 1929, the two-row tricycle version of the GP was available. It was the Model GPWT or GP Wide Tread of tricycle front wheel design with wide-set rear wheels and a front-mounted cultivator, a design similar to the popular Farmall. Deere equipped it with 24x4-inch (61x10-cm) tricycle front wheels and 44x10-inch (112x25-cm) rear steel wheels. The larger diameter rear wheels boosted the tractor's speed in fourth gear to 4⅛ mph (6.6 km/h). In 1932, the "improved" GPWT's hood was tapered at the back to aid visibility, and the steering was modified to an over-the-top configuration with better steering characteristics.

The Deere engineers also added a longer frame, higher operator platform, an adjustable cushion-spring seat,

spark and throttle levers mounted on the steering wheel support, and individual rear wheel brakes for shorter turns between row-pairs when planting or cultivating.

The John Deere General Purpose Wide Tread tractor of 1932 was advertised as having new and improved four-row planting and cultivating equipment. The Great Depression limited production of the last version of the GPWT to only 445 units.

Various versions of the GP Standard Tread were produced, including an orchard version, or GPO. Lindeman Manufacturing of Yakima, Washington, originated the GPO concept by lowering the tractor's profile. It later added track units to create a crawler GPO-Lindeman, or GPO-L. Only twenty-five GPO-L tractors were made, and only a few are known to exist today.

The GP Standard Tread stayed in the line until 1935. The GPWT was phased out in 1933 to make room for something dramatically better.

A narrow-tread tricycle John Deere GP potato series model with 68-inch (173-cm) tread to cultivate two 34-inch (86.5-cm) potato rows was made between 1930 and 1931. The P series was discontinued in 1931 when offset rear wheels were added to the wide-tread, or GPWT, version allowing it to handle the 68-inch tread needed for potato rows. Wayne Bourgeois restored this 1930 GP P, number P 5114.

A two-row cultivator was mounted in holes cast in the frame in the GP P and other tricycle versions of the GP. A side-mounted steering arm turned the front wheels.

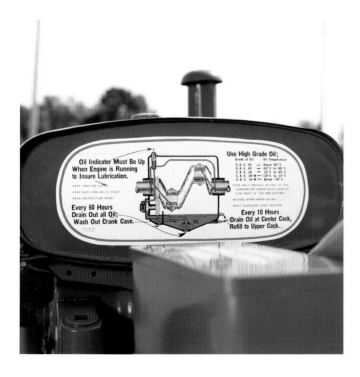

Tractor maintenance instructions on the operator's view of the fuel tank on the GP P.

Swinging the seat to the right or left adjusted the operator's viewpoint.

This 1933 GPWT with over-the-top steering was the final version of the last wide-tread series begun by John Deere in 1932. It has the lengthened frame, the tapered hood and fuel tank, an operator's platform above the rear axle, and an adjustable seat. This tractor, owned and restored by Verlan Heberer of Belleville, Illinois, carries serial number 404943 as the 167th one built. The depression limited production of the late-series GPWT to only 445 tractors.

Two 40- to 42-inch (102–107-cm) rows were spanned by the GPWT's long axles to allow cultivating two to four rows of corn, cotton, or other wide-spaced row crops. John Deere advertised the last version as the "improved" wide tread with "new visibility, new ease of steering and greater comfort for the operator."

A seat with a spring and adjustments put the operator of the later GPWTs high in the saddle for a good view of the working cultivator. Throttle and spark control levers were placed near the steering wheel for easy access.

The Improved John Deere
Shown with Inset Rear Wheels

—providing 68-inch tread for
Potatoes and Other Narrow-
Row Crops

The John Deere General Purpose Wide-Tread is a real cost-reducer in the growing of potatoes and other narrow-row crops. When used in these crops, the tractor is equipped with special inset rear wheels as shown at the left.

Equipped with a John Deere GP-240 Series Two-Row Cultivator, the tractor will cultivate from 15 up to 25 acres in a 10-hour day, doing better work than can be done with horses. Operating costs are lower than with other tractors because of the ability of this tractor to burn low-cost fuel.

Above: *John Deere made a potato tractor of the GPWT by installing inset wheels to reduce the tread to 68 inches (173 cm)—just what the spudmen needed.*

Left: *John Deere refined its row-crop tractor with the "Improved" GP of 1932. The GPWT could mount two- or four-row cultivators, and the driver sat high in the new seat for a better view. Large wheels boosted crop clearance. This is the pulley side of Verlan Heberer's 1933 Improved GPWT.*

DYNAMIC DEERE DUO

Deere's second-generation row-crop tractors would prove to be the company's all-time bestsellers. Quickening its climb up the learning curve from its early GP experiences, Deere introduced the Model A General Purpose two-plow tractor with many new features in 1934. The A was a tricycle row-crop tractor with a familiar John Deere kerosene-fueled, two-lunger power plant, but under the green-and-yellow paint it was new from the inside out. The A was driven by a 5½ x6½ -inch (140x165-mm) bore-and-stroke engine turning at 975 rpm. The tractor was rated for two 16-inch (41-cm) plows, and 1934 Nebraska tests showed 18.72 drawbar and 24.71 belt hp from its distillate-burning engine.

A four-speed transmission added to its utility with speeds of 2⅓, 3, 4¾, and 6¼ mph (3.7, 4.8, 7.6, and 10 km/h). Its new power lift had been converted from mechanical to hydraulic, and it both raised and "cushion dropped" mounted implements. The row-crop machine had infinitely adjustable rear wheel tread with wheel hubs sliding on long-splined axles extending from its one-piece transmission case, centerline draft, and differential brakes geared directly to the large drive gears. Overall, the A's new features made it a useful, easy-handling, and very efficient row-crop tractor.

The use of big 50x6-inch (127x15-cm) rear wheels gave the A the needed crop clearance under its rear axle without the need for drop gearboxes to add height as used on the earlier GP designs. The width of the rear wheels was adjustable to 56 inches (142 cm) for plowing, or out to 84 inches (213 cm) for straddling two 42-inch (107-cm) corn rows. The new A weighed about 3,525 pounds (1,600 kg) on steel wheels. New low-pressure pneumatic tires were soon available for the tractor.

Ease of maintenance was stressed in advertising brochures for the Model A. "The John Deere Model A can be serviced from a standing position," one brochure stated. "Under no condition does it become necessary to crawl under the tractor or lie on your back to get at parts. Because the valves and valve seats are located in the cylinder head it is an easy job to service this part of the tractor yourself on the farm," it said, thereby "servicing costs are extremely low because the average operator can do the work himself and save the cost of hiring a mechanic."

More than 292,000 Model As in various configurations were made from 1934 to the end of its production in 1952.

A year after Deere introduced the A, the company introduced a tractor aimed at replacing the last team of horses on the farm: the Model B. Advertised as being two-thirds the size of the A, the little B made 11.84 drawbar and 16.01 belt hp burning distillate fuel when first tested at Nebraska in November 1934. Its 4¼ x 5¼-inch (108x133-mm) engine turned at a more rapid 1,150 rpm, and the tractor's shipping weight was 2,763 pounds (1,254 kg). The Tricycle B came with 48-inch (122-cm) steel drive wheels in the rear and 22-inch (56-cm) tricycle wheels in front. It, too, was available with pneumatic tires. The B also had a long and successful production run: More than 306,000 Model Bs were made between 1935 and 1952, making it the most popular John Deere ever.

Specialized versions of both the A and B were produced, including the standard tread AR and BR models in 1935, and the orchard-equipped AO and BO with extended fenders, shielded fuel and water filler caps, shortened clutch, and lowered seat position. Wide-row versions were designated AW, narrow-row as AN, and high-crop-clearance models as ANH and AWH. The Model B was also available in similar specialized versions including a narrow-row, single-front-wheeled General Purpose model offered as a garden tractor to work vegetable truck farms or market gardens. Truck farms, or truck patches, are independent one-person operations with the garden produce both grown and sold at market "off the truck" by the grower.

A farmer at work on his 1937 Model A cultivating check-rowed corn.

The adjustable tread of big 50-inch (127-cm) rear steel wheels sliding on long-splined axles gave the new John Deere Model A flexible wheel spacing. This 1934 A was collected by the late Bill Ruffner of Bellevue, Nebraska. The two-14-inch plow rated A and its smaller companion, the Model B, were John Deere's all-time sales leaders.

Proudly cast into the rear axle housings of the Model A is the name that would popularize two-cylinder tractors among U.S. buyers. This 1934 model is not equipped with the new hydraulic power-lift that was available on the model.

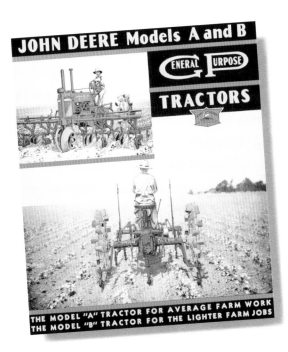

Early advertising for the steel-wheeled Models A and B show a four-row cultivator mounted on the A and a two-row hand lift on the B.

Six to eight horses were put out to pasture for every Model B John Deere sold, the company claimed. This 1936 B on steel wheels is equipped with a BB221 two row cultivator with "armstrong" lift. The B had the same features as the A but was only two-thirds its size. Don McKinley and Marvin Huber of Quincy, Illinois, restored this old tractor and cultivator to new life.

The lever at the right needed an operator with a strong back to lift the cultivator at row ends. A Power-Lift was an option, for an additional cost.

Above: *Splined axles with sliding wheel hubs made infinite tread adjustment possible.*

Left: *Detachable road rims kept farmers with steel-lugged tractor wheels out of trouble. Caretakers of early paved roads posted signs prohibiting their use by lugged vehicles. Road rims were removed before field work began. This 1935 B is owned by Wayne and Cindy Beckom of Kokomo, Indiana.*

Above: *The B was started on gasoline from this one-gallon (3.8-l) tank. Once running and warmed, the engine was switched to kerosene or distillate.*

Left: *John Deere offered rubber tires on the B from its introduction in 1935. In 1937, the B's frame was lengthened 5 inches (12.5 cm) to make it compatible with cultivators and other equipment made for the A. This 1936 model was restored by Dan Peterman of Webster City, Iowa.*

Standard tread and a compact profile marked the BR tractors. Electric starting and lights were options available from 1939. This 1939 model was restored by Robert Waits of Rushville, Indiana.

The first John Deere specialty crop B was the 1936 BW-40. Its tread could be set up for working rows as narrow as 20 inches (51 cm) or as wide as 42 inches (107 cm). This BW-40, serial number 2513, is the second of only six made. Bruce Aldo of Westfield, Massachusetts, owns this rare machine. It was originally shipped to the San Francisco, California, branch in October 1936, for use in the vegetable-growing area in the Sacramento Valley.

LOW-DOWN STREAMLINED AO

In 1936, the orchard version of the A was "streamlined" to become the Model AO Streamlined or AOS (as today's collectors call it). More streamlining was on the way. Deere ads touted the streamlined AO as a tractor "specially designed for grove, orchard, vineyard, and hopyard." The ad continued, "Notice the fully-streamlined, low-down design . . . the narrow compact construction . . . the short wheel base . . . the full enclosure of chassis, rear wheels, belt pulley, and flywheel . . . not a thing to catch branches, to injure blossoms, to bruise fruit. A real orchard tractor."

Streamlining before its time came with the John Deere AO Streamlined orchard model. Started in 1936 as an improved AO, the AOS was built low and narrow with fenders extending almost to the front hood. The "Stealth-like" design was from John Deere engineers, not from industrial designer Henry Dreyfuss, then at work styling the other John Deere tractors. This 1938 AOS is owned by Edwin Brenner of Kensington, Ohio.

Orchard work was the forte of this 1936 BO owned and restored by Bruce Wilhelm of Avondale, Pennsylvania. Its extra fender shielding and low profile helped it slip through orchards without damaging trees, blooms, or fruit. Citrus fenders that completely covered the rear wheels were available. This BO's polished brass nuts were not standard. They have been added for show.

BO-LINDEMAN CRAWLER

A track-type version of the B was the BO-Lindeman, or BO-L, introduced in 1939. As Deere & Company had done earlier with the GPO-L, Deere shipped the BO drive train to Lindeman Manufacturing in Yakima, Washington, where that company added its track units to create the little crawler. Built first to serve the orchardists in the fruit-growing areas in Washington State, the crawler tractor later gained some popularity in other regions of the United States. The BO-Lindeman was soon providing its sure-footed traction to Corn Belt farmers, to small timber cutters for snaking logs out of the woods, and to others who needed its light-footed grip. The crawler's flat tracks with their large surface area spread the tractor's weight over a bigger soil area thus reducing soil compaction. That flotation effect allowed track-type tractors to move over soft ground where wheel-type tractors would sink in and mire down.

The BO-Lindeman was rated as a three-bottom 14-inch (36-cm) plow tractor due to its superior traction and slower gearing—quite an accomplishment for a B-size tractor. Its four-speed transmission gave it ground speeds of 1¼, 2, 2¾, and 4 mph (2, 3.2, 4.4, and 6.4 km/h). Track shoe width was 10 inches (25 cm), and the track assembly added to its weight, topping out at 4,420 pounds (2,007 kg). Steering clutches disengaged one track at a time for steering. In May 1945, Deere bought the Lindeman company and soon began to make and assemble its own crawler tractors based on the Lindeman undercarriage, first in Yakima, then in a new Deere plant in Dubuque, Iowa.

Crawler tractors powered by John Deere power trains became available in 1940 when Lindeman Manufacturing of Yakima, Washington, began to install their track units on the John Deere BO chassis. This 1945 BO-L, or BO-Lindeman, was rated as a three-plow tractor. The late Donald Rogers of Atlanta, Illinois, collected this crawler. John Deere bought Lindeman in 1945 and used its track system as the basis for its own crawler tractors built in Dubuque, Iowa, starting in 1947.

Fairings on the BO hood kept filler caps from catching branches.

Lindeman track unit on the BO engine and transmission pioneered John Deere's own MC crawler, which debuted in 1948.

A Case for Rubber Tires

In the early 1930s, engineers at Midwestern agriculture colleges were testing and measuring the traction effects of pneumatic rubber tires on tractors. The trials showed a 20 to 25 percent gain in useable drawbar horsepower from rubber-tired tractors along with a 25 percent savings in fuel when used on heavy loads. Although the new tires added as much as $200 to the price of a tractor, they were soon in demand because of the increased productivity and comfort they offered. Also weighing heavily in favor of the new tires was that tractors so equipped could be driven down paved roads where their steel-lugged counterparts were banned (steel-lugged tractors were sometimes equipped with road bands circling the lugs, so they could venture onto the protected pavements without stirring the ire of the township road commissioner).

The As and Bs were the first of the John Deere tractors to be available on rubber tires, from the mid-1930s on. By 1938, virtually all farm tractors made in the United States could be bought with factory-installed rubber tires.

During World War II, rubber shortages caused a temporary return of some new tractors to steel wheels. However, synthetic rubber compounds developed during the war helped to get rubber tires back on tractors before the war's end.

At first, rear wheel weights supplied the extra weight needed for maximum traction on rubber tires. Farmers added weights to their rubber-tired tractors after research pointed out that it would reduce tire slippage. Early wheel weights included concrete disks cast with holes for mounting to tractor wheels. Manufacturers soon supplied cast-iron wheel weights. Later on, water, with calcium chloride added to prevent freezing, was injected into the tires to add the needed weight for best traction. Nearly all tractors tested at Nebraska on rubber tires had their weight supplemented by some method to reach their optimum performance level.

Above left: *Steel wheels were cut down and rims welded on to accept rubber tires. Montgomery Ward sold these knobby Riverside tires.*

Above right: *Pneumatic rubber tires helped the Model A and other John Deere models become more efficient tractors when they became available in the early 1930s. George Braaksma's restored 1934 Model A has factory French and Hecht wheels made for rubber tires.*

Above: *This 1937 gold-painted Model D helped the Kansas City sales branch celebrate John Deere's centennial that year. Collector Charles English, Sr., of Evansville, Indiana, learned of the special machine, traced it to Kingfisher, Oklahoma, and acquired it. The tractor had been in service in Kingfisher from 1938 to 1980. Starting with what he described as "the worst worn-out tractor I ever saw," English completely rebuilt the D, finishing it in a gold metallic paint that closely matched the original gold color.*

Left: *Charles English, Sr., displayed his restored, centennial-marking gold Model D at regional collector shows in 2000. The gold D bears serial number 131570.*

A 1938 Model G brochure.

THREE-PLOW MODEL G

Individual farm size increased even more as power farming boosted the productivity and efficiency of farmers. One man could do more work than ever before, and, with a larger tractor, more yet. The tractor folks at Deere saw a need for a bigger row-crop tractor for the larger-farm market. In 1937, they responded with the three-plow Model G. It resembled the A and B but had a stouter 6⅛x7-inch (155x178-mm) engine that Nebraska-tested at 20.7 drawbar and 31.44 belt hp at 975 rpm. It could pull a 10-foot (305-cm) tandem disk or easily handle four-row planters and cultivators. It was heavier than the A and B, too, weighing 4,400 pounds (1,998 kg).

Gearing was through a four-speed transmission that gave it working speeds of 2¼, 3¼, 4¼, and 6 mph (3.6, 5.2, 6.8, and 9.6 km/h). Its two front tricycle wheels were 24 inches (61 cm) in diameter and 5 inches (13 cm) wide. The G's rear steel wheels were 51½ inches (131 cm) in diameter and 7 inches (18 cm) wide. It, too, was soon rolling on rubber tires measuring 6x16 inches (15x41 cm) in front and 11x38 inches (28x97 cm) on the rear axle.

"The Model G will especially appeal to the large-acreage corn grower," John Deere ads claimed, "because of its ability to handle a three-bottom plow, large disk harrow, four-row cultivator, two-row mounted corn picker, and to provide ample and steady belt power for threshing, grinding feed, pumping and similar jobs." Growers of other crops were also targeted in the John Deere ads: "The large-acreage cotton grower will appreciate it because of its ability to handle three-row bedders under all conditions, and four-row bedders under many conditions, four-row planters and cultivators."

Power and weight were later increased, and a 1947 Nebraska test of the G on rubber tires resulted in 34.49 drawbar and 38.10 belt hp output. Available only in row-crop configurations, the Model G series was in production from 1938 to 1953, and more than 60,000 were sold.

Left: *A bold line forming a shield around the leaping deer was added to the 1936 John Deere trademark. The following year, an easier-to-stencil trademark replaced the 1936 trademark. The deer still vaults a log.* (Deere & Company archives)

Above: *Large-acreage corn growers got some big help when the Model G was introduced in 1937. The three-plow tractor was nearly as powerful as the durable D but as a row-crop design, the G could plant and cultivate four rows. The G's frame widened near the engine to make room for the big 6⅛x7-inch (155x178-mm) bore-and-stroke power plant. This 1938 G has the small radiator that was later replaced with a larger unit to cure overheating. Wayne Bourgeois of Kahoka, Missouri, collected this tractor.*

Left: *Heavy equipment, including four-row cultivators, were quickly hoisted by the G's hydraulic Power-Lift.*

Even a one-horse farm could get its own sized tractor in 1937 when the Model 62 was introduced. Designed to work in row crops, one row at a time, the 7-hp machine had the engine and drive train offset to the left and the driver's seat offset to the right, for increased forward visibility. After seventy-nine units were made, the Model 62 became the unstyled Model L. Professional tractor restorer Ron Jungmeyer of Russellville, Missouri, owns this 62, number 62-1048.

A "BABY" ONE, TOO

John Deere, still trying to replace those holdout teams hanging around on smaller farms, now went after the market on one-horse farms.

The year 1937 saw another tractor introduction, but on the lower end of the power spectrum: the Model 62. Seventy-nine Model 62s were built in 1937 before it was renamed the Model L utility tractor. The L was a small machine rated for one 12-inch (30-cm) plow—a vast departure from the other John Deere models of the day. It was powered with a John Deere–designed, Hercules-built vertical two-cylinder gasoline engine. Power output on tests was 7.01 drawbar and 9.27 belt hp from the 3.25x4-inch (83x102-mm) engine revving at 1,550 rpm. The little tractor weighed but 1,515 pounds (688 kg). The three-speed transmission provided speeds of 2, 3½, and 6½ mph (3.2, 5.6, and 10.4 km/h).

The L was built as a one-plow, one-row unit for small operators including truck farm vegetable growers. Innovative firsts for the series included the power train offset to the left on the axles, with the operator position offset to the right. That made for better forward and under-tractor visibility for careful cultivating of small plants in rows. A belt pulley was available, but no PTO was offered. The Model L differed from other John Deere tractors of the day in another way: It had a foot clutch instead of the familiar hand clutch of all of the other models.

The L was built in Moline, and the production of the new tractor there resulted in the formation of the Wagon Works Tractor Division that by 1943 was referred to as the John Deere Moline Tractor Works. Ira Maxon, Max Sklovsky, and Willard Nordenson were awarded patents in 1944 for some features of the L utility tractor. Ira Maxon was Max Sklovsky's son, and he was also a Deere engineer, as was Nordenson.

Styling, or streamlining, of the series came in 1939.

This 1938 unstyled LI in highway yellow was the industrial version of the L. This one is equipped with a No. 7 sickle-bar mower for mowing highway right-of-ways or other maintenance mowing. Ron Jungmeyer is the owner.

Later versions included the LA, with power increased by four horsepower and the rear wheels enlarged to 24 inches (61 cm) from the original 22 inches (56 cm), and the LI (industrial) version, which was painted highway yellow. Publicity for the larger LA models claimed an increase in power of about 45 percent and an increase in weight by about 700 pounds (227 kg), from 1,500 pounds (681 kg) to 2,200 pounds (999 kg), due primarily to the cast rear wheels, a solid base frame, and a heavier engine. Many LIs were equipped with belly-mount sickle-bar mowers for highway right-of-way mowing. Electric starting and lights were available from 1939 on. The L Series tractors were designed and built at the John Deere Wagon Works in Moline.

Deere's advertising for the Model L claimed it was "ideal for the small general farm, the spare-time farmer or the market grower. It can be furnished with belt pulley and a complete line of equipment to handle all small-farm

power jobs and give you the daily work out-put of 2 to 3 horses."

The unstyled Models L and LI were built from 1937 to 1938 with about 1,500 made. Only about 70 of those were the yellow-painted industrial version. About 9,840 styled versions of the L and 2,010 styled LI tractors were made between 1938 and 1946. Serial numbers indicate 12,475 LA models were made between 1940 and 1946.

THE SHAPE OF THINGS TO COME

Deere & Company now had a popular line of sturdy, economical tractors that had well served the company and helped its customers survive a devastating depression. Times were soon to get better, and so were the tractors, shedding their stodgy utilitarian shapes for a new progressive, even exciting, look.

CHAPTER 4

John Deere Style

Above: *A father greases his styled Model A while his son oils a miniature version in this painting by Walter Haskell Hinton entitled "Pint-Sized Shadow."* (Deere & Company)

Left: *A styled 1939 BNH owned by Tommy and Doris Jarrell of Wilmington, Delaware.*

A BNH operator had controls close to hand, another Dreyfuss innovation.

Pressed steel frame, an armchair seat with the battery below, standard electric starting and lights, and gas-only or all-fuel engines further improved the John Deere A and B models brought out in 1947. New clamshell fenders are installed on Bill Zegers's 1950 A. The gasoline engine boosted the tractor's drawbar pull to 34.14 hp in 1947 tests, making it a full three-plow tractor.

I n the mid- to late 1930s, the United States was trying to recover from the Great Depression that had devastated the nation's economy. With renewed hope for recovery, firms were eager to expand sales. At the same time, American industries were learning that styling products with new eye-pleasing shapes helped them sell. Industrial wares from cars to can openers were suddenly being redesigned to add aesthetically pleasing lines. Sleekness was to come even to farm tractors, replacing their knobby, utilitarian features.

In 1937, Deere hired noted New York industrial designer Henry Dreyfuss and his group to "style" the John Deere Model A and B tractors. The results of his firm's work with the tractor engineers in Waterloo culminated in 1938 with the introduction of the streamlined John Deere Model A and B tractors.

The tractors' appearances were transformed. Graceful sheet metal formed in curving lines covered the tractor top, from its radiator cap back through a new hood. The hood was tapered from front to rear giving the operator a better view forward for more accurate steering and precise row-crop cultivation. Horizontal slots, or louvers, starting from the newly designed tractor front, completely covered the radiator and the projecting front wheel pedestal to give the machine a new look of solidity and strength.

Not only was the Dreyfuss design team able to smooth and round out the lumps and bumps in the Deere tractor lines, but their design work also aided in the overall safety and usability of the machines. For example, coolant temperature and oil pressure gauges were clustered together on an instrument panel right in front of the operator. No longer did a tractor driver have to peer around the hood to check a gauge installed at some hard-to-spot location.

John Deere Waterloo engineers were also pleased to learn that the Dreyfuss styling team knew a thing or two about manufacturing. The industrial designers often had some very good ideas about easier and less expensive ways of making parts. Industrial design, Deere & Company learned, could pay off practically as well as aesthetically.

Deere & Company was so pleased with the results achieved by industrial designer Dreyfuss that the renowned firm has continued to make its mark on major John Deere products right up to the present day.

Industrial designer Henry Dreyfuss of New York applied this new stylish look to the family of John Deere A and B tractors that were introduced in 1938. This is a styled 1939 Model BNH, a narrow-row, high-clearance, specialty-crop tractor. With its single front wheel, big 40-inch (102-cm) rear wheels, and long rear axles, the BNH could be set up to cultivate as many as six 16-inch (41-cm) rows. Rear wheel widths could be adjusted in to a narrow 56 inches (142 cm) or out to a wide 104 inches (264 cm). Its crop clearance under the rear axle housings was 26 inches (66 cm), suiting it for work in tall-growing vegetable crops. Tommy and Doris Jarrell of Wilmington, Delaware, are the owners. Tommy restored this machine from its "basket case" condition. Only 446 BNH models were built.

HORSEPOWER BOOST, TOO

With its 1938 styling, the Model B got a larger 4½x5½-inch (114x140-mm) bore-and-stroke engine, as compared to the 4¼x5¼-inch (108x133-mm) engine on the unstyled models. That gave the B an increase in power from 11.4 drawbar and 16.01 belt hp to 16.44 and 18.53 hp respectively, as tested on rubber tires. The B also gained about 115 pounds (52 kg) moving it up to 2,878 pounds (1,307 kg).

The styled A got a horsepower boost in 1939 with an engine change that added ¼ inch (6.5 mm) to its engine stroke. Its power tests at the Nebraska test station went up to 26.2 drawbar and 29.59 belt hp when it was tested on rubber tires. That compares with 18.72 drawbar and 24.71 belt hp ratings in 1934 tests on steel wheels. The A also gained about 158 pounds (72 kg) in its transformation to a weight of 3,783 pounds (1,717 kg). Both the styled

A and B were equipped with six-speed transmissions featuring a two-lever design. One lever selected its three speeds forward and one in reverse. The second lever provided high-low ranges in the selected gear.

"If you are profit-minded . . . if you want to make more money . . . if you are interested in equipment that builds income by cutting operating costs . . . make it a point to inspect the great new John Deere Models A and B Tractors," read a 1938 Deere advertisement for the streamlined machines. "You'll like their modern styling, their pleasing appearance, and the unobstructed vision they give you—but even more important are the great money-saving values that only a careful inspection will disclose." Farmers did like the styled A and B tractors and made them the most popular Deere models ever.

Above: *The flywheel was totally enclosed on late A and B models, once the starter was relocated to the bottom of the tractor's main gear case. Engine controls were mounted on the left side of a new steering wheel pedestal.*

Right: *This ad for the new A suggests that "experience is the best teacher."*

Choice of the Tractor-Wise

WHEN it comes to determining tractor value, "experience is the best teacher." Thousands of today's John Deere owners know from personal experience with other tractors that you just can't equal a John Deere. These "value-shopped" before they bought, and thousands more who found that the exclusive John Deere "two-cylinder idea" really pays off in more dependable performance season after season . . . in fewer and far lower repair bills down through the years . . . in longer tractor life.

Equally important, these owners have found that John Deere's advanced engineering provides a greater combination of modern operating features to speed up every power job, do it better, make it easier.

The more you know about John Deere Two-Cylinder Tractors, the more convinced you'll be that a John Deere is the tractor for you. See your John Deere dealer for the complete facts and a demonstration of the size and type that fits your needs. Compare it on every count with any other tractor you could own. We feel certain you'll be on your way to more profitable, more enjoyable farming—with a John Deere. For free literature, fill out and mail the coupon below.

JOHN DEERE
Moline, Illinois

John Deere, Moline, Illinois   Dept. T438

The modernized B came with the same standard features introduced on the A. This 1949 B shows the enclosed flywheel, starter and lights, the cushy seat, and the pressed-steel frame common to the model. The improved B, introduced in 1947, had its drawbar horsepower for the gas tractor increased to 24.62 by a larger-bore engine turning 100 rpm faster.

Consistent with the increasing demand for more and more horsepower on Corn Belt farms, the Bs power more than doubled from an 11.84 drawbar hp tractor at its introduction in 1935 to a 24.62-hp machine just eleven years later. Its features evolved along with its power increases.

Above: *Its single front wheel, long axles, and dished large rear wheels made the BN adaptable to many different row spacings of high-growing vegetables and other crops. Its various configurations allowed the BN to replace the BNH and BWH in the specialty-crop lineup. This 1950 BN is one of Marysville, Ohio, collector Earl Scott's stable of narrow-row John Deere tractors.*

Right: *Large 42-inch (107-cm) wheels and tires gave the BN lots of crop-clearing height. Reversing the dished rims left to right gave the operator a choice of narrow tread rear wheel widths.*

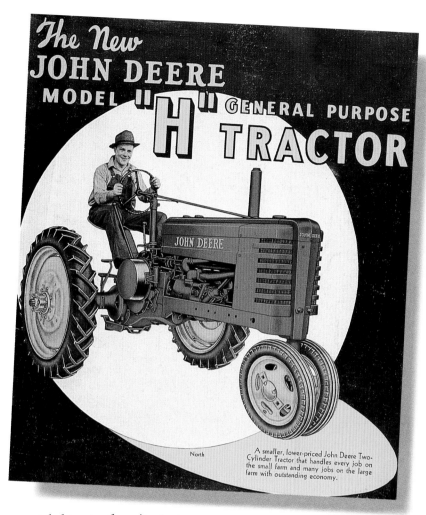

A smaller, lower-priced John Deere Two-Cylinder Tractor that handles every job on the small farm and many jobs on the large farm with outstanding economy.

North

The small Model H was a styled tractor from its start.

THE SMALL MODEL H

A new, smaller row-crop tractor, the Model H, replete in the new Dreyfuss styling, came out in 1939. It was a handy two-row tricycle-type machine resembling the A and B models, but was smaller with a 3.56x5-inch (90x127-mm) bore-and-stroke two-cylinder engine that turned over at a busy 1,400 rpm. The tractor, rated for one 16-inch (41-cm) plow, weighed but 2,063 pounds (937 kg). The belt pulley on the H ran off the camshaft rather than the crankshaft as on the larger John Deere models. That resulted in a higher pulley location and a reversed pulley rotation, compared with the other John Deere tractors. The H was available only on rubber tires and only with an all-fuel configured engine. It was equipped with a three-speed transmission with gears of 2½, 3½, and 5¾ mph (4, 5.6, and 9.2 km/h) forward and 1¾ mph (2.8 km/h) in reverse. A foot throttle allowed the engine to run at 1,800 rpm for a transport speed of 7½ mph (12 km/h) in third gear. Its 1938 tests at Nebraska showed the H produced 12.48 drawbar and 14.84 belt hp. It came on 8x32-inch (20x81-cm) rubber rear tires with 4x15-inch (10x38-cm) tires in front.

Deere also produced some specialized versions of the H. The HN model had a single front wheel for narrow rows. High-clearance versions, the HWH and HNH, were also available, providing 25 inches (64 cm) of under-tractor clearance for handling tall-growing crops, staked plants, and bedded plants. Rear pressed-steel rims, originally made for the Model B, were adapted to the HWH and HNH. Equipped with 38x8-inch (97x20-cm) rubber the big rims added about 4 inches (10 cm) to the crop clearance. Front ends varied between a single tire on the narrow-row tractor to wide-front, high-clearance axles on the HWH.

Still comparing tractor performance to horses, John Deere advertising claimed the two-row H could cultivate 25 to 30 acres (10–12 ha) per day compared with only 8 acres (3.2 ha) per day for a one-row cultivator pulled with a team of horses. "Now a tractor that will replace your animal power," declared an H advertising piece introducing the small tractor.

Deere sold the H, HN, HWH, and HNH from 1939 to 1947, achieving sales totaling about 58,600 for all models.

Above: *The Model H, a lower-priced, one-plow, tricycle row-crop John Deere, joined the growing tractor family in 1939. It carried through the new Dreyfuss styling applied a year earlier to the larger A and B models. The H only came on rubber tires. Front-mounted two-row cultivators combined with excellent visibility around the tapered fuel tank and hood made the H a favorite machine for cultivating row crops. It was also available in Models HN with single front wheel, HWH with wide front and high clearance, and the HNH with single front wheel and high crop clearance thanks to its big 38-inch (97-cm) rear wheels. Leonard Bruner of Rising City, Nebraska, restored this 1939 H, complete with its silk-screened logo on the hood sides.*

Right: *The pulling end of Bruner's 1939 H.*

Above: *The handy little H became even handier when electric lights and a starter were available. It started from the driver's seat with no more flywheels to fling. This 1945 H, with lights and electric starter, was given a new life when it was completely restored by its owner, two-cylinder expert Don Ward of Chula, Missouri.*

Left: *An ammeter joined the other panel instruments of the electric-start H.*

Single front wheel and large 38-inch (97-cm) pressed-steel wheels made this 1940 HN a narrow-row, high crop clearance specialist. Earl Scott of Marysville, Ohio, owns this HN with fenders.

A styled 1949 Model B owned by Bill Zegers of Newton, Iowa, exhibits the Dreyfuss touch.

Green Machines Meet the Man in the Brown Suit

New York industrial designer Henry Dreyfuss might have seemed an unusual choice when he was picked in 1937 to give John Deere tractors a modern look. Originally a stage designer for New York theaters, Dreyfuss had moved into the new field of industrial design beginning in 1928.

By 1936, his designs had remade the New York Central railroad's crack New York to Cleveland passenger train Mercury, into a streamlined "flying gray metal tube." He trumped that breakthrough in rail travel in 1938 with the bold transformation of NYC's flagship Twentieth Century Limited into another vision of railroad modernity, speed, and luxury.

It may have been Dreyfuss's streamlining of the steam locomotive's black utilitarian hulk in flowing shrouds of curvaceous sheet metal that in 1937 inspired young John Deere engineer Elmer McCormick to seek his help. The Deere & Company Waterloo tractor engineers knew they had a problem with the aesthetics of their Models A and B tractors and lacked the design savvy to solve their ugly problem. With grudging approval from Charles Stone, Deere's head of manufacturing, McCormick traveled to New York and contacted Dreyfuss. Stone wasn't enthusiastically convinced that stylists were needed for anything as down-to-earth as farm equipment.

But by September 27, 1937, the Dreyfuss design work was formally authorized. By November, a wooden mockup of the proposed new Dreyfuss design was shown at the Waterloo factory. Like the Dreyfuss-streamlined steam locomotives before them, the styled Models A and B were reborn by the design work. Bold radiator louvers began at the front of the radiator and swept back in a right-angle bend to the radiator shroud. The new hood was tapered from the rear to the front allowing better vision from the tractor seat.

Dreyfuss also promoted a new design of the typical John Deere pan seat with its "cheese holes" for drainage and ventilation. His alternative was declined by the conservative company. The old seat was good enough for a tractor.

The newly styled Model A and B John Deere tractors were introduced in 1938. Dreyfuss was awarded a design patent in November 1938 for the unified radiator cover and hood he had designed for the models.

Commenting on the design approach Dreyfuss used on the NYC passenger trains and the John Deere tractor projects, author Russell Flinchum noted the designer used an "abstract play between vertical and horizontal forms that resulted in a convincing image of power. The dominant vertical," he noted, "is balanced by flanking horizontal forms to give the illusion of movement while standing still." Flinchum chronicled the famous designer and his works in *Henry Dreyfuss, Industrial Designer: The Man in the Brown Suit.* Dreyfuss habitually wore conservative brown suits, Flinchum says, that reflected the Dreyfuss non-flamboyant business approach. Though he had a healthy ego, he avoided being a star.

Dreyfuss continued to distinguish himself in industrial design projects, working with a small but steady client list of major companies, including Deere & Company. Royal typewriters also got the Dreyfuss treatment. When secretaries complained of headaches caused by light reflecting off their typewriters' black shiny surfaces, Dreyfuss had them dulled down with non-reflecting paint that wrinkled as it dried. Hoover vacuums also got the Dreyfuss design treatment he sometimes called "cleanlining." Later in Dreyfuss's career, his team designed the Bell Telephone Model 500 phone, with the now-familiar rounded-outward shape that housed the dial, ringer, and handset cradle. Dreyfuss and his associates also later turned their attention to the Honeywell "round" thermostat, a product found today in almost every American home.

During World War II, he worked on many classified projects for the government including a six-week rush, hush-hush design and construction of a Situation Room for the Joint Chiefs of Staff in Washington, D.C. The room was designed to provide them with instant graphic war situation reports.

With his growing interest in "anthropometrics," or fitting machines to human dimensions and abilities, Dreyfuss worked on fighter plane cockpit layout during the war to design more fail-safe controls. That experience was expanded into his "Joe and Josephine" figures and their complex physical measurements. Joe and Josephine figures represented the range in physical dimensions of the people who would use the equipment he designed. His design intent was to assure operators comfort, safety, and convenience. He was able to use those studies in later work for Deere & Company.

Color renderings from Dreyfuss, dated 1940, published in Flinchum's book, show a John Deere tractor design with the general configuration of the Model M of 1947. The Dreyfuss early drawing shows the machine with the characteristic John Deere pan seat. Dreyfuss must have finally won his case with Deere on that comfort, safety, and convenience feature because the Model M (which the drawing unmistakably represents) was released with a rectangular padded seat—the first ever on a John Deere tractor. Joe and Josephine must have made their contribution to the M design and to all who operated that model and the many that followed.

By the 1950s, Dreyfuss was the leader in his profession, Flinchum claims. He had become the acknowledged conscience of American industrial design.

Dreyfuss endeared himself to clients by exhibiting total immersion in their design projects. He prided himself in operating the equipment he designed, including learning to sew while working on the Singer sewing machines, learning to type when working on Royal typewriters, and, yes, even learning to drive a tractor during the John Deere projects. He even kept a John Deere tractor at his South Pasadena,

California, home, Flinchum says.

The designer impressed clients by sketching his design ideas inverted during presentations so they emerged right side up as viewed by clients across the table as his prolific ideas flowed from his mind and out through his pencil.

Dreyfuss designs more than ever before fitted the tractor to the operator with the firm's work for Deere & Company on another major product, the New Generation of Power tractors in the late 1950s. A leading specialist in muscular-skeletal problems was brought in to help Dreyfuss design the seat on the tractor. Dreyfuss celebrated his design contributions to the machines at the introduction of the new tractors in Dallas in 1960. His partner, Bill Purcell, worked closely with Deere & Company on the New Generation machines.

Dreyfuss summed up his approach to design in his 1955 book, *Designing for People.* "We bear in mind," his introduction explained, "that the object being worked on is going to be ridden in, sat upon, looked at, talked into, activated, operated, or in some other way used by people individually or en masse. When the point of contact between the product and the people becomes a point of friction, then the industrial designer has failed. On the other hand," he concluded, "if people are made safer, more comfortable, more eager to purchase, more efficient—or just plain happier—by contact with the product, then the designer has succeeded."

Seeing the New Generation of Power tractors with their comfortable state-of-the-art posture seats must have given the great designer a warm feeling of accomplishment.

Dreyfuss died in 1972 at his home in South Pasadena.

FACELIFT FOR MODEL D

The rugged Model D got its styling "facelift" in 1939 in a design treatment that differed from that of the newer General Purpose tractors. Radiator bars on the D's grill were vertical rather than the horizontal treatment as on the A, B, and H models. The new Model D was tested at Nebraska in July 1940 on rubber tires and achieved 38.2 drawbar and 42.05 belt hp. The new styling didn't make it pull more, but its rubber tires did. The D also gained some weight in its transformation, showing up some 1,200 pounds (545 kg) heavier than the original model of 1924, with a final weight of 5,269 pounds (2,392 kg).

Styling of the Model D in 1939 modernized its looks and enhanced its reputation as a strong, sturdy tractor. This 1953 Streeter D was among the very last Ds built. Its serial number 191598 marks it as the twenty-ninth assembled of ninety-two Ds made in the street outside the Waterloo, Iowa, tractor factory in the summer of 1953. That outside-the-factory history gives it the "Streeter" nickname. Mike and Jackie Williams of Clinton, Iowa, restored this Rice Special that is co-owned by Joel Armistead of Adairville, Kentucky.

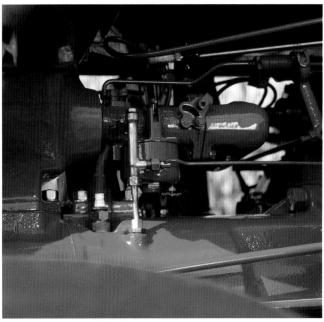

Above: *Power-robbing pre-ignition was controlled on the D with this water-injection plumbing. Water injected into the cylinder from the cooling system kept the fuel-air mixture in a hot, heavily loaded engine from igniting before the power stroke.*

Left: *The 1953 D was the last of a model in continuous production for nearly thirty years. Announced in 1923, the D was the first in a long line of John Deere "Johnny Poppers." By 1953, the D's drawbar horsepower had grown to 38.02 from only 22.53 hp at its initial Nebraska test in 1924. The big rice tires on this D suggest all of the mud and tough conditions this tractor survived during its working life.*

Styling caught up with the three-plow G in 1941 when it was updated as the new six-speed styled GM. It was built during only eight months of 1942 when wartime restrictions stopped its production. The GM was built again between 1944 and 1947. This 1945 GM, with electric lights and starter, was restored by its owner, Bill Zegers, a former John Deere dealer of Newton, Iowa. John Deere redesignated the GM as the Model G in early 1947.

RESTYLING THE MODEL G

Last to get the Dreyfuss styling was the row-crop-only tractor, the Model G. It was updated as the six-speed styled GM in 1941. It was available with electric lights and starter. Due to a wartime freeze on prices for existing models, the GM became a new model rather than just a styled G. The only way they could work within the Office of Price Administration (OPA) rules then current and not lose money on the tractor was to introduce it as a new model at a higher price. The GM on rubber tires weighed 5,100 pounds (2,315 kg) compared with 4,400 pounds (1,998 kg) for the original G. Rubber tires on the GM were available as 6x16 inch (15x41 cm) on the front and 11x38 inch (28x97 cm) on the rear.

Tractor model introductions were nearly curtailed at John Deere during the war years as the factories and engineering departments concentrated on defense work. The GM model designation was dropped after wartime restrictions were lifted, and, by 1947, the GM model had reverted back to the Model G designation, with its streamlining and other features intact.

The non-solenoid starter on the GM took a hefty left foot "boot" to pop off its two big cylinders.

Side-by-side placement of the air intake and exhaust stack characterized the styled G and GM models as on Zeger's 1945 model. The G that was revived in 1947 stayed in production until early 1953. An armchair seat with the battery below replaced the pan seat in mid-1947 when the G got electric lights and starter as standard equipment.

The "V for Victory" salute is exchanged by the overall-clad lady tractor driver with soldiers passing in an army truck convoy in this patriotic wartime painting by Walter Haskell Hinton. John Deere factories hummed with defense projects during the war while tractor production nearly stopped.

THE G HI-CROP

The 1947 model year also marked the introduction of the first of the John Deere super-high-clearance tractors, the Model G Hi-Crop. Throughout its production life, the Model G came only in an all-fuel version and was made only in General Purpose row-crop wheel placements of single front wheel for narrow rows, wide front for row crops, and double narrow wheels tricycle front.

When tested again at Nebraska in 1947 on rubber tires, weighted to 7,442-pounds (3,379-kg) the Model G proved 34.49 drawbar and 38.10 belt hp, besting its 1937 drawbar test on steel wheels by about 25 percent.

In 1943, John Deere advertising stressed patriotism above specific products. During World War II, women assumed more hands-on jobs on farms as well as in factories producing war materials. Anticipating the war's end, this ad suggested readers set aside some of their war bonds to buy new farm equipment.

THE M

An aggressive stance by the company under president Charles Deere Wiman after World War II moved Deere & Company into a new period of expansion.

Wiman had succeeded William Butterworth in 1928. With a mandate from the board of directors to make a low-cost tractor in a new location on a waterway, Deere bought land in January 1945 and erected a factory on the Mississippi River in Dubuque, Iowa. By mid-1947 the factory was producing the Model M, a brand-new utility tractor.

The John Deere M was influenced by a milestone tractor from another manufacturer. In 1939, Henry Ford reentered the tractor business in the United States after an eleven-year hiatus. Ford introduced a revolutionary two-plow, 16-drawbar hp Ford tractor with a new Ferguson System of equipment mounting and hydraulic control. The internal-hydraulics-controlled equipment was attached integrally to the tractor by way of a rear three-point hitch. The little two-plow utility tractor with row-crop capabilities was both cheap and highly productive. It was an immediate success and sold some 10,000 units in its first six months of production. By the time the John Deere Model M came out, 600,000 of the little gray Ford-Ferguson tractors had already been sold. That now-famous Ford 9N revolutionized tractor design, especially in hydraulic implement control and attachment of implements with three-point hitches.

John Deere carefully mimicked the Ford product as to size and operation but held on to its own ideas as to engine configuration. By the time the M was in full production, Ford had ended its connection with Ferguson and was making its own Ford Model 8N tractor set apart with its light-gray sheet metal and red-painted castings. The John Deere M was of similar four-wheel utility design but had its engine and drive train offset to the left to improve cultivation visibility on the right side of the tractor as it straddled one row. The company offered some twenty different Quik-Tatch mounted implements for the M.

A rectangular padded seat for the operator was a welcome addition to the new line of John Deere M tractors. The Dubuque-built machine came out as a standard-tread general purpose utility tractor. The first of a new line of vertical-engined tractors, the M's upright 4x4-inch (102x102-mm) gasoline-fueled engine ran at 1,650 rpm—one of the fastest-turning engines Deere had made to that time. As first tested at Nebraska, the M rated 14.39 drawbar and 18.21 belt hp. By October 1947, the M produced 18.15 drawbar hp and 20.45 belt hp to compare favorably with the Ford 8N's 20.85 drawbar and 25.5 belt hp.

The M's four-speed transmission recognized the need for speed in transport and provided a 10 mph (16 km/h)

road speed in fourth. Working speeds were 1⅝, 3⅛, and 4¼ mph (2.6, 5, and 6.8 km/h). Front tires were 4x15-inch (10x38-cm) and the rear were 8x24-inches (20x61-cm). The M weighed 2,560 pounds (1,162 kg).

The M was joined by the tricycle version Model MT in 1949. The MT was a little heavier at 2,900 pounds (1,919-kg) and rolled on two tricycle-spaced 5x15-inch (13x38-cm) front tires and larger 9x34-inch (23x86-cm) rear tires to give it additional crop clearance. Both the M and the MT had Touch-O-Matic hydraulic controls for integral-mounted implements. The MT's dual system could be set to raise and lower front or rear cultivator gangs at the same time, or right and left sides independently. The M was built from 1947 to 1952 and the MT from 1949 to 1952. More than 40,500 Model Ms and 25,800 MTs were made.

Charles Deere Wiman, nephew of Charles Deere, became Deere & Company president in 1928. As director of manufacturing beginning in 1924, he pushed for tractor improvements and the development of John Deere combines and corn pickers. He continued to press those projects during his 1928–1955 presidency. Burton Peek, was interim president during World War II while Wiman served in defense positions in Washington, D.C.

Above: *The new Model M for smaller farms arrived after World War II.*

Left: *Convenient hydraulic implement control was the hallmark of the new John Deere M general-purpose utility tractor series brought out in 1947. Made in a new Deere factory in Dubuque, Iowa, it led a new line of smaller tractors powered with a new vertical, in-line, two-cylinder engine. Bill Zegers of Newton, Iowa, restored this 1948 M and its No. 32 blade. The M introduced John Deere's Touch-O-Matic hydraulic system that offered precise control of the rockshaft for implement depth adjustment.*

Rear trailing arms mounted and lifted integral equipment on the Model M. Horsepower tests pegged the output of the busy 1,650-rpm, 4x4-inch (102x102-mm) engine at just over 18 hp at the drawbar. The M soon replaced Waterloo-made John Deere tractors in its power category.

Drop gear arrangement gave the M general-purpose utility the crop clearance needed to cultivate row crops.

MC CRAWLER STARTS A DIVISION

Brother to the M and MT was the first Deere-designed and -manufactured crawler, the Model MC. John Deere had supplied Model BO chassis since 1939 to the Lindeman factory in Yakima, Washington, and the Lindeman Company used the chassis to build their crawler, the BO-L, for use in the sloping orchards of the area. In May 1945, Deere acquired Lindeman and, in 1949, built its own track-type tractor based on the same vertical engine used in the M and MT tractors. The MC crawler and the industrial version of the M, the MI, became the basis for Deere's industrial division that later grew up in Dubuque.

In 1950, Nebraska tests of the new MC crawler showed 18.3 drawbar and 22.2 belt hp. The MC's track-type design allowed a 4,226-pound (1,919-kg) maximum pull compared with only 2,329 pounds (1,057 kg) for the rubber-tired Model M. The MC's four-speed transmission provided users with a slow 0.8 mph (1.3 km/h) in low gear, 2.2 mph (3.5 km/h) in second, 2.9 mph (4.6 km/h) in third, and a not-so-fast 4.7 mph (7.5 km/h) in fourth gear. The MC had track shoes in widths of 10 or 14 inches (25 or 36 cm) available. Tread widths available were 36 or 42 inches (91 or 107 cm).

Deere advertising positioned the small crawler as "The compact, powerful economical Model MC, for use wherever extra flotation is needed . . . in light soils, wet, loose ground, rough terrain, woodlands, etc."

About 6,300 of the MCs were made between 1949 and 1952. Deere stopped manufacturing the MC in 1952.

CREATURE COMFORTS STANDARD

After World War II, Deere began making electric starting and lights standard equipment on tractors. Powr-Trol for hydraulic control of pulled implements was also available from 1947 on. Roll-O-Matic, a feature that averaged out the bump one front wheel received from the other, became available on tricycle front ends. Deere & Company described it as "knee-action."

High-compression versions of the A and B tractors, designed to burn gasoline, became available in 1947. Conversion kits to change older models to burn gasoline instead of kerosene were also available from Deere. The gas-burning Model A produced another 4 hp on the drawbar, while the Model B added 3 drawbar hp when running on gas.

There were other changes afoot on farms, especially in the Corn Belt. Scale of operations had continued to grow, and farmers were clamoring for even more productivity. As before, Deere was up to the challenge.

Showing its versatility as a utility tractor, Ron Jungmeyer's 1948 M mounts a No. 30 loader. The M had electric lights and starting as standard features.

The John Deere trademark was redesigned in 1950 with its leaping deer antlers angled up and to the front. The log was missing and a legend, "Quality Farm Equipment," was added. (Deere & Company archives)

The 1950 brochure for the new MT, or M Tricycle.

CHAPTER 5

Soaring Horsepower

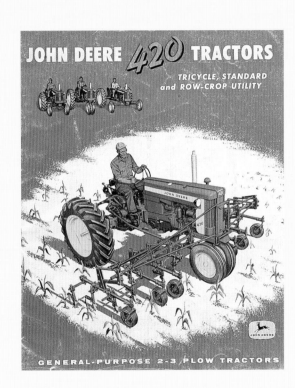

Above: *Brochure touting the Deere 420 models.*

Left: *A 1953 Model R restored by David Walker of Chillicothe, Missouri.*

U.S. farms began to specialize and to grow in scale after World War II. Many general farms in the eastern Corn Belt states were rapidly converting to cash-grain farms, where crops were all sold off the farm rather than fed to a farmer's livestock. Operators were removing their pasture fences and planting larger fields "fence row to fence row." The affordability of chemically based fertilizers, especially nitrogen, allowed Corn Belt farms to buy that element, rather than grow nitrogen in legumes through a four-year crop rotation. Without the need to grow nitrogen-fixing legumes such as alfalfa and clover, formerly fed as hay to cattle, farmers could eliminate their farm animals and sell grain off the farm. Labor shortages associated with the war and good grain prices also encouraged farmers to sell their livestock and specialize in crops grown on extensive acreages. To speed up their time-critical tillage work in planting season, farm operators increasingly became interested in more powerful tractors.

DIESEL DEERE

The development of a diesel tractor led John Deere Waterloo engineers into previously uncharted territory. They began work on a diesel project as early as the fall of 1935 with the realization they would have to solve many problems, including that of starting a diesel engine in cold weather. The extra-high compression in the diesel engine and its ignition by the heat of compression worked against each other in cold temperatures, especially when using the low-volatility diesel fuels injected into the cylinder at the start of the power stroke.

When the engineers couldn't get their 24-volt electric starting system to work on the test power unit, the engineers turned to an auxiliary two-cylinder gasoline engine, which worked well enough. After solving that problem, they continued to develop the rest of the tractor beginning with eight models built and tested in 1941. By 1944, the original design had been improved, and five better machines were made. By 1947, a new lot of eight further-improved big diesel standard tractors were built and tested before final changes were made and the Model R was introduced.

JOHN DEERE MODEL R DIESEL TO THE RESCUE

Introduced in 1949, the big R was the first John Deere diesel and the company's first tractor boasting more than 50 hp. The R was a standard-tread machine, the eventual replacement for the venerable Model D. Its hefty 5.75x8-inch (146x203-mm) diesel operated at 1,000 rpm and produced 45.7 drawbar and 51 belt hp in its Nebraska tests in April 1949. A small, electric-start two-cylinder opposed gasoline starting engine put the R's 16-to-1 high-compression diesel into motion and helped warm the engine to start-up temperature.

The tractor weighed 7,400 pounds (3,360 kg), and its 7.5x18-inch (19x46-cm) front and big, broad, 14x34-inch (36x86-cm) tires on the rear helped keep it on top of the ground. Weight added for testing brought it up to 10,398 pounds (4,721 kg), and the big machine showed a maximum pull of 6,644 pounds (3,016 kg) in Nebraska tests. The R also set a new fuel-efficiency record during the testing with 17.63 horsepower hours per gallon (4.58 hp hours/l) of fuel at rated load and 15.57 horsepower hours per gallon (4.05 hp hours/l) at varying loads. Fuel efficiency became a concern as engines got larger, so engineers measured and calculated the horsepower hours of work each gallon of fuel produced in the tractor under test. That figure could then be used to compare the relative fuel efficiency of same size or different size tractors.

A five-speed transmission moved the R along at 2⅛, 3⅓, 4¼, 5⅓, and 11½ mph (3.4, 5.3, 6.8, 8.5, and 18.4 km/h). Reverse was 2½ mph (4 km/h). A powerful and efficient tillage tractor, the R found an eager market among Corn Belt farmers as well as in the farmers of wheat country. More than 21,000 of the Model Rs were produced between 1949 and 1954.

"It's full speed ahead to bigger profits . . . with the John Deere Diesel," boasted ads at the R's introduction. The ads claimed fuel costs of eight cents per acre (0.4 ha) plowing with a five-bottom plow. Fuel savings of $900 per 1,000 hours of operation were claimed, compared with gasoline tractors of equal power.

Productivity, too, was emphasized in the ads, including touting the R's ability to pull multiple hookups of equipment, enabling a farmer to do more fieldwork in less time.

The R also introduced new styling to the Deere line. Deere again turned to industrial designer Henry Dreyfuss for the styling treatment. The new radiator grill design was of vertically pleated, or fluted, perforated metal capped with Deere's familiar tractor hood. The 1/16 -inch (1.6-mm) perforations, combined with the extra area provided by the pleated grill, permitted sufficient cooling air to pass through but kept chaff from plugging the radiator core. The grill could be quickly cleaned of accumulated chaff by a few quick finger swipes running down the grooves.

The R styling was soon to be seen on the next series of tractors Deere introduced: the Numbered Series.

Brochure announcing the first John Deere diesel tractor.

John Deere's first diesel and its first tractor with more than 50 belt hp was the 1949 Model R. Its other firsts included live independent PTO with its own clutch. That feature gave it live hydraulics, too. Larger-than-standard rear tires gave it more grip for antique tractor pulling contests in which its restorer, David Walker, competed.

Deep-treaded rice tires and single-rib front tires equip this 1951 R for work in dreadfully muddy conditions. Owner-collector Chad Reeter of Trenton, Missouri, put his R back in show shape with the help of neighbor and fellow collector, Mel Humphreys.

Above: *The four-spoke steering wheel brands this R as one built without power steering. Its five-speed transmission gave it a speed for every need.*

Right: *Wheat growers saw this ad for the R in their regional papers.*

Corn Belt farmers rigged tandem hitches of their tractors in the 1950s to maximize horsepower. This rig pulls a five-bottom plow and trails a clodsmasher to hurry along spring tillage. More powerful new tractors followed in the 1960s. (Photograph © J.C. Allen & Son)

Farmer Innovations

With few big tractors available from manufacturers in the late '40s and early '50s, inventive farmers began to cobble up their own by having local mechanics add power to older tractors with engine transplants from automobiles, innovations that sometimes greatly taxed the capabilities of the original tractor machinery. Many old Farmall 20 and 30 tractors met their glorious end with Ford V-8 auto engines whining away in their frames.

Another power-packing ploy used by farmers in the post-war period was tandem-hitching, or "piggy-backing," tractors by attaching two tractors in line, with the rear unit's front attached to, and pushing on, the front unit's rear. The result was twice the power, with but half the labor needed to operate the contraption, compared with running two tractors separately. Gas pipes and universal joints extended from the front tractor to let the driver steer from the rear tractor's seat. Rods or ropes allowed the clutch on the leading tractor to be engaged or disengaged by the operator in the rear. The control extension arrangement was reminiscent of rigs used on tractor-drawn grain binders to permit tractor operation from the binder seat as tractors replaced horses in the mid-1920s.

By the mid-1950s, some farmers began to buy kits from outside makers to turbocharge their tractor engines. These "blowers" jammed in more combustion air, to burn more fuel to produce more power. In many cases the add-on turbochargers did indeed boost power, but, in addition, they almost always voided the tractor manufacturers warranties because of the possibility of burning up an engine.

All of these "souped-up" machines sent a clear message to the tractor manufacturers: Farmers needed more powerful tractors, and tractor manufacturers quickly got the hint.

THE NUMBERED MODELS RAISE THE HORSEPOWER ANTE

Introduction of new models in all sizes accelerated after the war, especially in the early '50s when tractor production had finally caught up with demand, and tractor manufacturing and sales became more competitive. Higher horsepower and more features were now the game.

The first of John Deere's Numbered Series tractors was introduced in 1952. The Models 50 and 60 were worthy replacements for the well-known Models A and B. New sheet-metal styling with small vertical grooves in the radiator screens, as first seen on the R in 1949, helped give the Numbered Series its distinctive look. But their beauty was more than skin deep. The new 50 and 60 models both received a power boost of about 15 percent compared with their lettered predecessors.

Duplex carburetion (basically a carburetor for each cylinder) helped increase performance by providing the cylinders with a uniform mixture of fuel and air. Eyebrow ridges over intake valves provided the engines with Cyclonic Fuel Intake, meaning the fuel and air going into the cylinder was swirled together for more uniform combustion and extra fuel efficiency.

Their "All-Weather" manifolds had adjustments for optimum running in cold or hot weather. The new engines could be equipped to run on liquefied petroleum (LP) gas and "all-fuel" configurations in addition to gasoline. The improvements gave "faster starts, snappier response, smoother operation at all throttle settings, outstanding fuel economy, and prolonged spark plug life," according to John Deere promotional literature.

The power takeoff (PTO) operated independently of the transmission or transmission clutch to provide continuous, or "live," power for drawn implements. Hydraulics were also improved to continuous, high-pressure Powr-Trol, which operated independently of clutch or PTO for faster lift of heavier equipment. Dual Touch-O-Matic hydraulics allowed all-together or one-at-time lifting and lowering of front- and rear-mounted cultivator gangs.

Factory-installed (but optional) power steering in 1954 and rack-and-pinion adjustment of rear wheel tread were industry firsts. The latter, introduced with the Numbered Series, made adjustment of rear tread width a matter of loosening a few bolts and moving the wheel to the needed setting by means of a wrench driving a pinion gear working in slots in the axle. The new power steering used built-in hydraulics and soon became standard on the series.

Operator convenience was also addressed in the Numbered Series with longer hand-clutch levers and extended throttle levers, putting them closer at hand. The tractors also provided an adjustable seat backrest.

First tested on gasoline in 1952 at Nebraska, the Model 60 showed 36.9 drawbar and 41.6 belt hp from its improved A-sized engine, the drawbar horsepower testing 2.76 more than the Model A. The 60 was tested at a weight of 7,413 pounds (3,366 kg) compared with its 5,300-pound (2,406-kg) shipping weight. The 60 came with 6x16-inch (15x41-cm) tires in front and 11x38-inch (28x97-cm) rubber on the rear drive wheels; it was available as an orchard tractor beginning in 1953. The 60 was offered in gas, all-fuel, or LP versions. Some 64,000 60s were eventually sold.

The smaller Model 50 was Nebraska-tested in 1952, burning gasoline and weighted to 5,349 pounds (2,428 kg) for a showing of 27.5 drawbar and 31 belt hp, or 2.88 more drawbar hp than the Model B it replaced. The Model 50's shipping weight was 4,435 pounds (2,013 kg). The tractor came on 5.5x16-inch (14x41-cm) front tires and 10x38-inch (25x97-cm) rear tires. The 50 was available in gasoline and all-fuel versions, and more than 33,000 were made from 1952–56.

"These heavy-duty, two-and three-plow tractors offer you many new operating advantages," John Deere ads claimed, "that will save time and speed up every power job on your farm . . . that will save work and make your farming easier than ever before . . . that will greatly increase the operating efficiency of your equipment and boost profits."

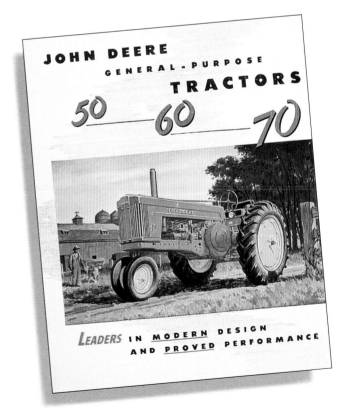

The 1953 brochure for the new Numbered Series tractors.

More power, more comfort, and increased usefulness were featured in a new line of numbered John Deere two-cylinder models that began to arrive from the John Deere tractor factories in the early 1950s. The 40 was to replace the M, the 50 the B, the 60 the A, and the 70 the G. And there were even more to come. This collection of Numbered Series tractors belongs to Bob and Mark Hild of Webster City, Iowa.

Farmer Bob Hild bought this 1954 Model 60 new in October 1954, when he returned from Korea to the corn, soybean, and hog farm he operates near Webster City, Iowa. More than forty-six years later the 60 holds a place of honor in his stable of restored John Deere tractors. The Model 60 was the first of the John Deere Numbered Series shipped from the Waterloo factory in early 1952. Hild's gasoline 60 has the optional power steering, fenders, live PTO, and high-capacity Powr-Trol hydraulics. More than 61,000 Model 60s were built.

Above: *Modifications of the engine to a two-barrel, or duplex, carburetor design gave the 60 more power than the A it replaced. The 60 was built on a cast frame instead of the pressed-steel frame used on the late As. Rear-wheel tread was adjusted with an optional rack and pinion arrangement on the hub and axle. A six-speed transmission was shifted with a single lever. The 60 became a worthy replacement for the tried and tested A.*

Left: *This magazine ad in 1954 featured the new John Deere factory-engineered power steering.*

Above: *The new 801 three-point hitch, could transfer some draft resistance into extra weight on the drive wheels. The early three-point design was available on the 50, 60, and 70 models. Baldwin's 60 LP carries this hitch.*

Left: *Liquefied petroleum, or LP, became a fuel choice on the new John Deere Numbered Series tractors in 1953. This 1954 standard 60 has that option as well as power steering, rice tires, and deep clamshell fenders. Ford Baldwin of Lonoke, Arkansas, collected this rare machine. Only 25 were made. It is shown on the edge of an Arkansas rice field.*

Above: *Its new family styling also dressed up the smaller Model 50. Longer hand clutch levers on the Numbered Series models made them easier to work. The throttle handle was also lengthened to move it closer to hand. The 50 came with basically the same equipment that was on, or could be optioned on, the larger 60 model. It was first shipped in the summer of 1952. By the end of production in 1956, more than 32,000 units of the Model 50 had been made. Bob and Mark Hild restored this 1955 nifty 50.*

Right: *Modern features of the Numbered Series are shown in this cutaway brochure art.*

Above: *Over-the-hood visibility was improved on the Numbered Series by putting the air intake under the hood, thus eliminating the air intake stack of earlier models, and by moving the exhaust stack to the right side of the hood. The live hydraulic system got more capacity to handle bigger loads faster.*

Left: *Advertisements for the Numbered Series models featured their capacity and economy.*

137

The four-to-five-plow Model 70 replaced the G starting in 1953. This 1953 70 LP row-crop, owned by Bob and Mark Hild of Webster City, Iowa, is equipped with a mounted No. 813 moldboard plow. Fuel options on the 70 model grew to include gasoline, all fuel, LP, or, after the fall of 1954, diesel.

THE MODEL 70

The Model 70 John Deere joined the Numbered Series in 1953 as the replacement for the G. The 70 was offered in gasoline, all-fuel, and LP versions. Later in 1954, the 70 became available with a diesel engine, making it the first John Deere diesel row-crop tractor. Nebraska tests showed 44.2 drawbar and 50.4 belt hp for the 70 gasoline, and 45.7 drawbar and 51.5 belt hp for the 70 diesel. The shipping weight of the 70 was 6,035 pounds (2,740 kg) for gasoline and all-fuel tractors. The LP version was heavier at 6,335 pounds (2,876 kg), and the 70 diesel even heavier at 6,510 pounds (2,956 kg). They were Nebraska-tested with 1,800 to 2,700 pounds (817–1,226 kg) of weight added to optimize performance. The 70 Series row-crop tractors came with 6x16-inch (15x41-cm) tires in front and 12x38-inch (30x97-cm) tires in the rear.

Several different front and rear axle versions were available, as were Hi-Crop models for those growers needing high-clearance capabilities. The 60 and 70 were also made as standard-tread models. Between 1953 and 1956, Deere manufactured about 43,000 of the Model 70s.

A special double-wide rear seat was used by dealers to field demonstrate to prospects the features of this 70 LP with its integrally mounted implements.

The LP fuel option adds the cylindrical high-pressure tank shape to the profile of this 70 LP owned and restored by Bob and Mark Hild. Hild's Numbered Series John Deere collection includes this 70 LP with a mounted three-16-inch No. 813 moldboard plow and the necessary rear-wheel and front-end weights to make it an efficient plowing machine.

John Deere's first diesel row-crop was the 70 diesel, introduced in September 1954. This restored 1956 model, owned by Ed Hermiller of Cloverdale, Ohio, has a shiny non-factory muffler. The 70 diesel set new fuel efficiency marks when it was tested in Nebraska in October 1953, toppling the R from that throne. It was a popular Corn Belt tractor with enough power to work fast and efficiently through heavy tillage duties, spring ground preparation and planting, and then finish the stretch in rapid-paced four-row cultivation. Production of the 70 model surpassed 41,000 units.

Top: *The 70 diesel used a new V-4 gasoline starting motor that replaced the two-cylinder starting motor design used in John Deere's first diesel, the R.*

Bottom: *The 1954 brochure for the Model 70 diesel.*

A boost in engine speed from 1,650 up to 1,850 rpm added 15 percent to the power of the new 1953 Model 40 Series tractors from the Dubuque factory. The Model 40 Series replaced the Model M tractors. This 1953 tricycle 40N has a single front wheel for working narrow-row crops. Jeff Underwood of Dahlonega, Georgia, collected this tractor. It was photographed in front of an overshot water mill near Cleveland, Georgia.

THE 40S

Upgraded versions of the Dubuque-made Model M were introduced in 1953 as numbered models. They were the 40 Standard, the 40 Tricycle, and the 40 Crawler. They also wore the new vertical grill treatment of the 50, 60, 70, and R models. Improved hydraulics and other systems on the 40s were similar to those on the larger 50, 60, and 70 tractors. Horsepower was also increased by about 15 percent compared with the earlier Ms. Drawbar hp was up to 22.9 and belt hp to 25.2 in its tests. The 40 crawler sported either four- or five-track rollers, depending on needed track length. It showed 20.1 drawbar hp and 25.0 belt hp at Nebraska. The 40 Series was produced between 1953 and 1955.

Dual Touch-O-Matic live hydraulics allowed left and right or front and back cultivator gangs to be raised or lowered individually on the Dubuque-built Model 40 Series tractors. The 40 models included the 40 Standard, 40 Tricycle, and the 40 Crawler designs.

Above: *The 1953 Model 40 Tricycle was a handy-sized, two-row cultivating tractor on many smaller farms. This restored 40 Tricycle belongs to Mark Hild of Webster City, Iowa. He and his father, Bob, restored the tractor.*

Right: *The 1952 brochure for the 40 Series.*

Above: *An aspiring Hi-Crop, this 1955 model 40V Special was a high stepper. Crop clearance was an impressive 26½ inches (67 cm) on the vegetable special, compared with 32 inches (81 cm) on the 40 Hi-Crop. Only 328 copies of this configuration were made. Professional restorers Ken and Dan Peterman of Webster City, Iowa, restored this rare tractor back to its like-new condition.*

Left: *Model 40 tractors had advanced live-hydraulic systems that gave load and depth control of its three-point mounted integral equipment. Twenty-three rear-mounted and four mid-mounted implements were sold by John Deere for use on the two-plow tractor. Nearly 49,000 model 40s were manufactured.*

The largest John Deere tractor became more powerful in 1955 as the new Model 80, after engineers revamped its engine and features. Increased cylinder bore and a higher engine rpm, backed up with a new heavy crankshaft running in three main bearings, let it produce 61.8 drawbar hp compared with 45.7 hp on the R. Mel Humphreys of Trenton, Missouri, owns this spotless 1955 Model 80 that he and neighboring collector, Chad Reeter, restored.

THE STRONGER MODEL 80

Continuing to meet the demand for more horsepower in its largest tractor, Deere replaced the R with the Model 80 in 1955. Its diesel-only power was boosted by about 35 percent compared with the R, making it a full five-plow tractor. A new six-speed transmission gave it a wide range of working speeds. Helping to get the 80 diesel started on cold mornings was a new V-4 gasoline starting engine that revolved at 5,500 rpm. The 7,850-pound (3,564-kg) Model 80 had three sturdy main crankshaft bearings. The tractor produced 61.8 drawbar and 67.6 belt hp in its Nebraska test in 1955, coming from its bigger 6.12x8-inch (155x203-mm) bore-and-stroke two-lunger engine turning at 1,125 rpm. Test weight of the Model 80 was 11,485 pounds (5,214 kg). It was upgraded from the Model R to include the same hydraulic systems and live PTO as the smaller John Deere Numbered Series models.

"The Model 80 Diesel," John Deere literature bragged, "brings you big capacity at rock-bottom operating costs . . . is a powerful new John Deere Tractor with the brawn to plow a *six-foot [1.8-m]* strip . . . to handle *twenty-one feet [6.4 m]* of double-action disk harrow . . . to pull *double* hookups of hydraulically controlled field cultivators, tool carriers, rod weeders, grain drills. Here's capacity that will greatly increase your daily work output—that may even save you the cost of a second tractor and driver." The 80 was produced in numbers approaching 3,500 in 1955 and 1956 before it was again improved and introduced as a new model.

With no slackening in farmers' demands for more horsepower in their tractors, John Deere met the challenge of the 1950s with a growing family of new models with even more power, more color, and new three-digit model numbers.

Live PTO and live high-capacity Powr-Trol hydraulics gave the new Model 80 many of the features of the other Waterloo numbered model series. It also got a six-speed transmission to give its bigger engine more speed ranges for pulling the wide tools it could handle.

Above: *The brochure for the Model 80.*

Left: *Factory-installed power steering, convenient controls, a larger fuel tank, and operator comfort features helped stretch out the 80's work day to increase its total productivity.*

Used from about 1956 forward, this new stylized leaping deer trademark was registered in 1962. (Deere & Company archives)

The source of "Greatly Increased Power" was explained in this brochure.

THE TWO-TONE 20 TRACTORS

Even more power and style marked the new 20 Series introduced by John Deere in 1955. Horsepower jumped by about 20 percent above the power of the previous Deere line in each of the six sizes offered in the new series. The power boost was a result of increasing by ¼ inch (6.5 mm) the bore of the engine up to 4¼ inches (108 mm), increasing the compression, and adding an improved carburetor. And with additional yellow trim, there was no problem mistaking the new three-digit models for the two-digit, all-green numbered models they replaced.

The flashy two-tone 20 Series had, in addition to yellow on the wheels, more yellow as an accent stripe running along the hood then continuing down the sides of the radiator shroud. Thirty basic models in six power sizes were offered in the new series.

THE WATERLOO "BOYS"

The Waterloo-made 520, 620, 720, and 820 tractors replaced the 50, 60, 70, and 80 models. The tractor line had new engines that featured improved cylinder heads and pistons that increased combustion-chamber turbulence, resulting in more complete combustion. Power output and fuel efficiency were markedly increased, and the 20 Series set five new fuel economy records during their Nebraska tests. The John Deere engineers had once more succeeded in tweaking even more horsepower and fuel efficiency from their two-cylinder engines, engines first designed some thirty years earlier.

The 20 Series also had live PTO, which permitted the operator to continue the PTO in operation whether the tractor was stopped or in motion. Optional Float-Ride seats, which allowed adjustment of the rubber, torsion-spring suspension for the weight of the operator, were available. A universal three-point hitch with Custom Powr-Trol was also available, providing two speeds for either lifting implements or adjusting implement depth. Power-adjusted rear-wheel tread setting was another welcome option. "Just loosen three clamps and set the handy stop at the spacing desired," said the sales folder, "Then get on the tractor, ease in the clutch, and presto! . . . engine power slides the rear wheels in or out to the position selected."

The 520 was rated at 25.63 drawbar and 32.38 belt hp. The 620 measured up at 34.34 drawbar and 42.79 belt hp, and the big 720 passed the 50 mark with 40.63 drawbar and 50.67 belt hp.

In 1956, the 820 diesel, now called the "Green Dash" by collectors, replaced the 80 as the "big gun" in the line. The 820 first ran on a Model 80 engine, but in 1957, the Model 820 was offered with a more powerful engine. The improved "Black Dash," as that 820 is now called by collectors, pulled 69.66 drawbar and 75.60 belt hp in its 1957 test at Nebraska. With its extra power, the 820 moved up to a six-plow rating. The largest John Deere tractor of the day harnessed its strength through a six-speed transmission, allowing working speeds of 2⅓, 3½, 4½, 5¾, and 6¾ mph (3.7, 5.6, 7.2, 9.2, and 10.8 km/h), with a transport speed of 12½ mph (20 km/h). A "creeper" gear of 1¾ mph (2.8 km/h) was an option. The 820 shipped at 7,850 pounds (3,564 kg) but carried about two tons (1,800 kg) more weight at testing.

The 820 line offered a Rice Special, equipped with deep-tread rice tires, extra shielding for brakes, and beefed-up bearing protection for its often-muddy mission.

A power increase of 20 percent was part of the news about the new 20 Series John Deere models released in the late 1950s. Smallest of the Waterloo-built tractors brought out in 1956 was the Model 520, available only as a row-crop tractor with either tricycle or wide adjustable front. It replaced the numbered Model 50 tractors. Farmer-collector Don Rimathe of Huxley, Iowa, restored this sparkling 1957 Model 520.

Above: *New Custom Power-Trol, new adjustable Float-Ride Seat supported with an adjustable torsion rubber spring, and an independent foot-operated PTO, were well-received features on the series. Roll-O-Matic fronts were also available on the tricycle row-crop versions.*

Left: *Extra yellow trim marked the hood sides and radiator shroud on the 1956–1958 John Deere 20 Series tractors. A compression boost and an increase in engine speed by 75 rpm brought the gasoline-burning 520's drawbar horsepower to 34.31 from 27.5 on the Model 50. The 520 was a three-plow tractor.*

Above: *Sleek, flowing lines let this 1958 620 Orchard LP scoot through the fruit trees barely rippling the leaves. The 620 model had more power than the Model 60 it supplanted and was considered a full four-plow tractor. In its October 1956 Nebraska tests, the gasoline 620 showed 44.16 drawbar hp. Well-known John Deere collector Verlan Heberer of Belleville, Illinois, and his body man, Rick Scheibel, put the shine back in this treasure. With serial number 6216262, it is one of only ninety-two of its kind that were made.*

Right: *"Modern Hydraulic Functions" on the new series were illustrated in this brochure.*

Above: *In addition to its swift-looking orchard dress, the 620 was made as a standard-tread, row-crop tricycle, wide-front row-crop, and as Hi-Crop versions in all three fuel options. Its 20 percent power increase came from engineering tweaks, including another 150 engine rpm and a new combustion chamber shape that increased turbulence and added to power and fuel efficiency. The 620 model was the last two-cylinder orchard tractor John Deere made.*

Left: *The operator's seat put the 620 OLP driver down low behind the cowling shield.*

The big 720 row-crop led its field for power down the rows and brought new high fuel efficiency marks to John Deere. The diesel harnessed 53.66 drawbar hp from its two-cylinder power plant. Chad Reeter and Mel Humphreys of Trenton, Missouri, restored this sharp 1957 Model 720 to pristine condition.

The full five-plow 720 was the most powerful row-crop tractor on the market, John Deere advertising proclaimed. All four fuel versions of the 720, gasoline, diesel, all-fuel, and LP engines, produced more than 58 belt hp each in tests. This is Chad Reeter's 1957 tricycle 720 diesel.

Custom Powr-Trol introduced on the 20 Series featured a position-responsive rockshaft. The operator could set a precise working depth and return to that setting after raising and lowering the implement. The exclusive Load-and-Depth Control kept implements working at their pre-set uniform depth. It automatically transferred some implement weight to the drive wheels in tough pulls by raising the implement just enough to keep forward progress constant. Reeter's tractor also shows the new Float-Ride seat, universal three-point hitch, and optional power steering.

Above: *The distinguishing black dash on the Model 820.*

Left: *Most powerful of John Deere's 20 Series was the 820, worthy successor to the 80. The "Green Dash" 820 came out in 1956 with few differences from the 80 model except for its extra yellow trim paint and wider rear fenders. The improved "Black Dash" Model 820 came out in mid-1957 with its more powerful diesel engine producing 69.66 drawbar hp in its October 1957 Nebraska tests. Belt output was measured at 75.6 hp. This 1958 "Black Dash" 820 is owned by collector-expert Don Ward of Chula, Missouri.*

Above: *A brochure featuring five variations of the Model 420.*

Right: *The inside story of the Model 420 in a 1956 brochure.*

Dozer-equipped Model 420 Crawlers were a favorite of small contractors and builders. This 1956 crawler is in the collection of James Proctor of West Chester, Pennsylvania. Tested drawbar pull was 24.12 hp from the 4.25x4-inch (102x108-mm) bore-and-stroke gas engine. The 420 wheeled tractors pulled 27.08 hp from their vertical inline two-cylinder engines.

1958 Model 420 Crawler has LP fuel option. Randy Griffin of Letts, Iowa, owns this crawler equipped with a subsoiler-ripper.

THE DUBUQUE 20 MACHINES

The Dubuque 20 Series tractors, announced in 1955–56, became a fleet of many configurations. They included a small tractor, the 320, rated as a one-to-two-plow tractor with the same hydraulics of the other models. It replaced the Model 40 and matched that previous tractor's power output. The 320 came as a standard or utility tractor configuration.

The 420 was a step up in power from the Model 40 and was made in tricycle, standard, Hi-Crop, utility, wide-tread, low-profile, and in four- and five-track-roller crawler versions. It had a four-speed transmission with operating speeds of 1⅛, 2¼, 3, and 7¼ mph (1.8, 3.6, 4.8, and 11.6 km/h). A fifth gear was optional. A continuous-running independent PTO operated by a two-position foot clutch was available on the 420. Horsepower of the 420 was measured at 20.31 drawbar and 24.83 belt in Nebraska tests.

NO LONGER CONTENT

From the early postwar period to 1956, Deere & Company had moved its John Deere tractor development into high gear. More models with more power and efficiency were the result.

Engineering work started during World War II resulted in the M model design meant to take on all competitors for the small-farm market. Hydraulic systems not only lifted implements but controlled their depth settings. And mounting implements integrally to the tractor was adopted with Quik-Tatch.

Deere's first diesel tractor marched from its expanding tractor factories in 1949 to be followed shortly in 1952 with new numbered model series tractors that replaced the old lettered model tractors. In that proud series was the first diesel row-crop. Then just four years later, in 1956, the company introduced a broad new line of 20 Series models with big boosts in horsepower and functional features.

Deere & Company's action in the postwar recovery decade demonstrated that it was no longer content to build the same machines year after year. It was moving toward the future at an accelerating pace. What lay up the road?

Hydraulic controls on right fender of 420 Crawler.

Model 420C brochure of 1957 extolled its virtues.

CHAPTER 6

The Last of the "Poppers" and a New Generation of Power

Above: *The John Deere insignia on the front of a 1959 Model 730 owned by Steve and Lewis Schleter of Princeton, Indiana.*

Left: *A 1965 Model 4020 owned by Tom Manning of Dallas Center, Iowa.*

The world couldn't know, but the 30 Series, introduced in 1958, was to become the last of John Deere's famous line of two-cylinder tractors. There were major changes underway, but those new developments were a tightly guarded secret known only at Deere & Company—and within Deere only by those who needed to know.

Of course, Deere & Company couldn't stop making and selling tractors to wait while its clandestine project matured. So Deere kept its secret, improved its then current tractor line, and introduced the retooled line in late 1958 as the 1959-model-year 30 Series.

1958 brochure touting the new 30 Series tractors.

THE 30 SERIES

Since the engines had all been upgraded in the 20 Series, they remained the same and were not tested at Nebraska in the 30 Series tractors. New features aimed at operator comfort and ease of use were the hallmarks of the new series. A new deep-cushioned seat positioned the operator between two new flat-top fenders with built-in dual lights. A new dash design tilted the engine instrument panel upward, providing a better view for the operator. Rounded hood tops with more yellow trim and gentler bends tended to make the styling of the series a little friendlier than the earlier 20 Series. John Deere ads also noted the 30 Series tractors were easier to start, easier to shift, and quieter to the ear—the latter a contribution from the series' new oval-shaped (in cross section) muffler.

The 30 Series also featured a new steering wheel position. The steering column emerged from the dash, positioning the wheel at an angle for more-comfortable steering. This also made it easier for the operator to mount the tractor in front of the rear wheel. Gone was the need to climb over or around rear-mounted equipment to get into the driver's seat.

From the Waterloo tractor plant that year came the 530, 630, 730, and 830 models and their derivatives. The 730 diesel was available with optional electric start. That starting option had first been offered on late 720 diesels and became popular on the 730 diesels.

The Dubuque-made tractors, still using their vertical two-cylinder engines, included the 330 and the 430 models available in a wide variety of tread and axle configurations, as well as the crawler 430C.

The Model 435 diesel was the last two-cylinder model introduced by Deere, in June 1959. It was not a typical John Deere tractor for its day, since it was powered with a General Motors two-cylinder, two-cycle diesel engine. The 435 was the first small diesel tractor John Deere manufactured.

The 435 diesel was also the first John Deere tractor tested at Nebraska given a PTO horsepower rating rather than belt horsepower. More use was being made of the PTO on tractors and less use was found for belt pulley applications, so the change to PTO testing was a logical progression. The diesel 435 was available as a row-crop utility tractor with either 540- or 1,000-rpm PTO with industry standard specifications. The two-cycle 3.87x4.5-inch (98x114-mm) bore-and-stroke diesel hummed at 1,850 rpm and put out 28.41 drawbar and 32.91 PTO hp in its Nebraska tests in September 1959.

The beginning of the end for John Deere's two-cylinder tractors was the Model 530 introduced in 1958. The 530, which replaced the 520, continued the firm's small row-crop tractor power slot first held by the Model B in 1935. New to the model were flat-topped fenders housing dual-beam lights, and an upward angled steering wheel punctuating a new sloped instrument panel. Ken Smith of Marion, Ohio, owns this 1959 Model 530 equipped with wide 48–80-inch (122–203-cm) adjustable front axle. Its engine was the same as in the 520, and the gas versions produced 34.31 drawbar hp, making it a three-plow machine.

Minnesota John Deere two-cylinder collectors Gerald Holmes and Ron Coy add scale to their 1959 630 Hi-Crop number 631292. Their rare, all-fuel tractor, provided 32-inch (81-cm) under-axle clearance for working staked tomatoes, sugar cane, and other high-growing crops. Hi-Crop versions were available in 430, 630, and 730 John Deere models. Holmes and Coy found this tractor's rusting remains in eastern Florida and restored it to this top-notch shape.

Above: *The next step up in the 30 Series power range was the 630. With enough power to handle an integral four-bottom plow, the 630 was considered a heavy-duty tractor with power to fill the needs of medium- and large-acreage farms. The 630's gas engine produced 44.16 drawbar hp. All-fuel and LP versions were also available. This 1958 model was collected and restored by Doug Bockey of Spencerville, Ohio.*

Left: *A deep-cushioned seat with an adjustable backrest added to the driving comfort of the 530. Its new angled steering wheel placed it in a more holdable position. The new instrument panel clustered its gauges conveniently around the steering column.*

Above: *Large Corn Belt farms made good use of the big 730 diesel row-crop machines; it was among the most popular of the 30 Series tractors. Five-plow power let it rip through prime tillage, quickly work down and plant fields, then cultivate up to six rows at a time to wage war on weeds. It was also available as a tricycle, Hi-Crop, and as a standard-tread version. Diesel-engined 730s provided 53.66 hp of pull at their drawbar. Steve and Lewis Schleter of Princeton, Indiana, own this 1959 730 with adjustable wide front axle.*

Right: *Front end weights on the side and front helped counterbalance heavy rear-mounted equipment on the 730. Direct electric starting was an option on the 730 diesel. The 730s were available in four fuel options.*

Standard-tread 730s, like this 1959 model, were popular in grain-growing areas. Professional restorer-collector Dick Bockwoldt of Dixon, Iowa, owns this one.

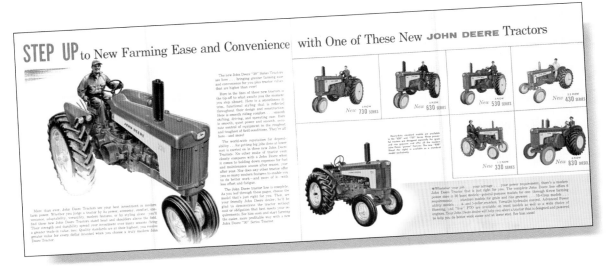

Six power sizes in the new 30 Series "ease and convenience" tractors were featured in the 1958 brochure.

Above: *Enormous 23.1x26-inch (58.7x66-cm) deep-treaded rear rice tires helped the 830 Rice Special tractor pull its nearly five tons and its huge loads through soft rice fields. Single-rib front tires helped with directional control. Peterman's 830 has the direct electric start option powered by a 24-volt electrical system.*

Left: *The 830 diesel, built between 1959 and 1960, was the largest Johnny Popper. The six-plow 830 produced the same power as the "Black Dash" 820s, 69.66 drawbar and 75.6 belt hp. It offered optional direct electric starting, or V-4 gasoline motor starting. This 1960 Rice Special 830, number 8305876, was made "new" by professional restorer-collector Ken Peterman and his son, Dan, of Webster City, Iowa.*

John Deere kept its small utility tractors viable in 1959 with the Model 330 and 430 Dubuque-made tractors derived from the earlier 320 and 420 Series of 1955–1958. This rare 1960 low-profile John Deere 330 Utility is owned by Suzanne Burch of Sikeston, Missouri. Only 247 were made. The 330 used the 4x4-inch (102x102-mm) vertical two-cylinder engine from the earlier Model 40. Drawbar horsepower was 22.4. Angled steering wheel, and the more aggressive use of yellow trim, were first seen on later 320 models. The angled panel and more taper to the hoodline were 30 Series changes.

Options, including the three-point hitch, made the 330 Utility a very versatile machine.

Extra under-axle clearance was provided on the 330 Standard compared with the utility version. Bill Burch of Sikeston, Missouri, owns this 1960 Standard 330. It was a one-row, one-to-two-plow tractor with 21 inches (53 cm) of crop clearance. With only 844 of this model made, it, too, is relatively rare. The 430 Series Dubuque tractors were powered with a larger two-cylinder 4.25x4-inch (108x102-mm) bore-and-stroke engine turning at 1,850 rpm. The 430 model iterations included standard (S), utility (U), two crawlers (C), row-crop utility (RCU), Hi-Crop (H), special (V), and tricycle row-crop (T) versions.

Above: *The 435 diesel was derived from the 430 row-crop utility into which the GM two-cycle diesel was installed. Jungmeyer's 435 has a three-point hitch, fenders, and spin-out adjusting rear wheels. The 435 was manufactured from the end of March 1959 until the end of February 1960.*

Right: *The John Deere 435 diesel was the very last of the company's U.S.-made two-cylinder tractors. More interesting than its historic niche though, is that the 435 was powered with a non–John Deere engine. Its powerplant was a General Motors 2-53 diesel two-cycle, two-cylinder engine. With its distinctive two-cycle hum, the tractor tested 28.41 drawbar hp and put out 32.91 PTO hp in its Nebraska tests in September 1959. The 435 model was the first time John Deere had used a diesel engine in its smaller tractors. Professional restorer-collector, Ron Jungmeyer of Russellville, Missouri, did the restoration on his 1959 Model 435.*

A huge surprise to John Deere watchers in 1959 was the enormous, eight-plow, four-wheel-drive Model 8010.

A Peek at the Future

A hint of things to come was the surprise unveiling of a massive four-wheel-drive Model 8010 tractor at a John Deere new model introduction show at Marshalltown, Iowa, in the fall of 1959. The new big green machine had a company rating of 150 drawbar hp from an engine capable of 215 hp. It could pull a mounted eight-bottom plow at 7 mph (11.2 km/h) and then lift the plow at the row end and turn sharply back into the next furrow. Articulated power steering with air brakes aided its control. With the ballast it needed for plowing, the awesome machine weighed 12 tons (10,900 kg). The message was clear: If it was power the American farmer desired, John Deere could supply it.

An updated version of the 8010, the 8020, came out in 1960 with an eight-speed Syncro-Range transmission, an oil-cooled clutch, and other improvements. The Syncro-Range transmission featured constant-mesh gears permitting "on the go" shifting between high and low forward speeds in each of four speed ranges. The transmission provided a total of eight forward and three reverse speeds as well as a stationary park position. Only in the park position could the engine be started or another gear range selected. The transmission was to serve well on later tractor models.

Somewhat ahead of its time, neither version of the eight-plow tractor sold well. But the time would come for such big tractors.

New Generation of Power

The world learned August 30, 1960, what the Deere engineers had been doing for the past seven years. That date marked the unveiling of the New Generation of Power tractors in Dallas, Texas.

The new machines were first introduced to dealers at "Deere Day in Dallas," a splashy, Texas-sized show staged at the Cotton Bowl with a huge barbecue and Al Hirt's New Orleans Jazz Band. Deere flew in a crowd of more than 6,000 people for the showing. The large scale of the event befit the importance of the introduction.

Forbes magazine called the all-new tractors "John Deere's boldest venture in its 124-year history." On the morning of August 30, the entire new line was on display in the Cotton Bowl parking lot. At noon in downtown Dallas, Stanley Marcus, president of premier retailer Neiman-Marcus, unwrapped a gem-garnished 3010 next to his jewelry counter with Deere president, William A. Hewitt, presiding over the event. Hewitt, Deere's sixth president, had taken over from his father-in-law, Charles Deere Wiman, in 1955, and would serve as CEO until 1982. The new tractor series was one of Hewitt's first steps toward his goal of modernizing Deere & Company.

At the same time John Deere dealers and the press were getting their first peek at the revolutionary new tractors in Dallas, semi-trucks were plying highways all across the United States transporting the disguised machines to John Deere dealerships. Just as the first press reports of the Dallas event were being released, the new tractors were ready to be shown to soon-to-be-impressed customers.

Announcing the New Generation of Power tractors, this brochure ended years of secrecy.

Above: *William Hewitt became Deere's sixth president in 1955 after the death of his father-in-law, Charles Deere Wiman, the corporation's fifth president. Hewitt moved the company into the modern era. He was president until 1982.* (Deere & Company archives)

Left: *John Deere New Generation of Power tractors shook up the industry with their far-reaching improvements when they were introduced in August 1960. These two tractors are part of that history: They carry the first serial numbers assigned to the 3010 and 4010 diesel tractors. Farmer-collector Ken Smith of Marion, Ohio, collected these row-crop tricycles—prime examples of the New Generation machines and their far-reaching improvements to tractor design.*

Under-wraps shipments to test sites in covered vans of the evolving prototype New Generation tractors helped keep the new models secret during their seven-year development. This 1960 restored 3010 diesel is the first with a production serial number.

Secret Shipments in Unmarked Trucks

Two of the first tractors destined for field test near Laredo, Texas, were crated and shipped from Waterloo in March 1956 in an unmarked Reo truck. The old Reo, grinding its way to the Texas test site, began to lose power and limped into Waco, Texas, debilitated by a burned valve. As project engineer Wendell Van Syoc later noted, "Here I was, entrusted with a big Deere & Company secret and was stalled in a public place." Fortunately, a quick cross reference search showed that a John Deere Model B tractor valve was the right size, but was too long to fit in the Reo. He bought the needed

valve from the local John Deere dealer and had a machine shop cut it to length and grind in a keeper groove. The Deere part worked fine in the Reo, and soon the old truck delivered the secret machines to Laredo with no one the wiser.

Subsequent test tractors were shipped in closed vans, Van Syoc recalls. "Doors were locked in Waterloo with keys available only in Waterloo and in Laredo, Texas. On arrival at the test site the truck driver was escorted to a coffee shop. After the tractors were unloaded and put in hiding, the driver was returned to his truck."

POWER SIZES FOR ALL USES

Very little about the New Generation tractors resembled the earlier John Deere models except for the flat-topped fenders with their built-in lights, first used on the 30 Series tractors, and, of course, their well-known green-and-yellow colors.

Except for these cosmetic similarities, the Models 1010, 2010, 3010, and 4010 were all new from front to back and top to bottom. They represented the most radical changes in the Deere tractors since the A and B models first appeared in 1934 and 1935.

Tractor weight concentrated on the rear wheels, a proven John Deere concept, was achieved in the new tractors by keeping the new engines to the rear of the frame, close to the transmission, differential, and drive axle. The lighter components, such as the large-capacity fuel tank and the radiator, were up front. All-new vertical four- and six-cylinder gasoline, LP, and diesel inline engines powered the line. Deere's venerable line of two-cylinder Johnny Poppers was nearly completely replaced in a single stroke.

The new four-cylinder 3010 and six-cylinder 4010 were equipped with what Deere called variable-speed engines. High horsepower-to-weight ratios gave the new line of tractors the advantages of higher operating speeds with a smaller percentage of their available power needed to move the tractor. Not only was the new line more powerful, but it was also more efficient. The 4010 produced 73.65 drawbar hp but weighed less than 7,000 pounds (3,178 kg). The 3010 diesel pulled more than 50 drawbar hp and was a full four-plow tractor.

Added to their other firsts, the new series of tractors provided closed-center hydraulics for live implement-raising "muscle" in three circuits. Power steering and power braking were also served by the new variable-displacement pump working from a common reservoir of hydraulic fluid. Eight-speed Syncro-Range transmissions, first available on the 8020, matched power and speed to job demands.

The rakish design of the front of the new tractors suggested constant forward motion, even when the machines were stopped. The front's dramatic angle evoked the mental image of a horse leaning into its harness as it moved ahead, or the camera-distorted old photos of race cars lunging forward as they sped down the track. It was a dynamic design indeed.

The carefully rounded and sculpted top engine cowling projected over the prow of the tractor then carried its arched line back to the raised instrument panel and its centrally located steering column and wheel. That made the operator's new posture seat seem a part of the whole machine. Engine cooling radiator intake screens with familiar fluting were well back from the front on both sides just ahead of the engine compartment. The filler cap up top in the front where the radiator was usually found was painted red. What was the fuel tank doing up front? These visible features hinted there was something powerfully different inside, as well as outside, these new tractors.

Other power sizes in the series were the 1010 with 30 hp at the drawbar and the 2010 with up to 40 drawbar hp. The 1010 was of utility configuration but with adjustable front and rear tread to handle row-crop work. The 2010 was offered in tricycle row-crop and row-crop utility versions.

In 1962, the 1010 and 3010 were offered as orchard and grove models. That same year, the big 5010 standard-tread tractor was announced. It was the first two-wheel-drive tractor producing more than 100 drawbar hp, measuring 105.92 drawbar hp and 121.12 PTO hp at Nebraska.

Earning power of new tractors keyed tractor information.

All-new four-cylinder gasoline, diesel, and LP engines powered the revolutionary 3010 models introduced by John Deere in 1960. Power of more than 54 drawbar hp placed the 3010 in the four-plow league. The 3010s were made available as row-crop tricycle, standard, row-crop utility, and as orchard versions. Innovations included closed-center hydraulics which provided instant power on demand in three "live" circuits to handle power steering, a rear rockshaft, remote cylinders, and power brakes. This is Ken Smith's 3010. The modern styling of the new tractor series suggested forward movement of the tractors even while they were at rest. In addition to the radiator, engineers placed the fuel tank near the tractor's front. John Deere's new eight-speed Synchro-Range transmission on the 3010 and 4010 models allowed on-the-go shifting up or down in each of two speed ranges. The Dubuque-made 2010 models offered similar styling and features but with engines of about 40 drawbar hp they ranked as three-plow tractors.

Above: *Its big six-cylinder diesel, gas, or LP engine, made the 4010 the standout model of the New Generation tractors. More than 73.65 drawbar hp was created in the new tractor that had a shipping weight of less than 7,000 pounds (3,150 kg). Company engineers called that a high-horsepower-to-weight design. That meant a smaller percentage of available power was needed just to move the tractor. Such a design allows higher operating speeds with less engine strain and better efficiency, they said.*

Right: *Features of the New Generation tractors, as on this 4010 diesel, included a new three-point hitch with lower-link sensing, a quickly convertible 540/1,000-rpm PTO, a new posture seat, and flat-top fenders. Many such revolutionary design concepts marked the new model.*

Above: *For the first time ever on tractors, the 3010 and 4010 provided power brakes, made possible by the design of the closed-center hydraulics.*

Left: *Operator comfort was a part of the New Generation tractor design. This scientifically designed posture seat on the 4010, was rail mounted to slide back and up to clear the platform to allow the operator to stand to change position. Hydrostatic power steering also helped to relieve operator strain by giving improved steering control. Less bending and reaching for shift levers was achieved by building them into the dash in front of the operator.*

This 1962 4010 LP Hi-Crop, number 23933, gave the vegetation it tended plenty of room and its driver a lofty perch. Sibley, Iowa, farmer-collector George Braaksma, restored this rare machine. It is the ninth one made of a total of seventeen, he says, and one of only five known to still exist. This one was found in Louisiana where it had been used in sugar cane production.

Young Ted Braaksma shows the high clearance of his Dad's 4010 LP Hi-Crop.

UNDERCOVER DESIGN, TESTING, AND MANUFACTURE OF THE NEW GENERATION

After a seven-year secret gestation period, John Deere had leapfrogged the competition with its New Generation of Power, a stunning new tractor series far ahead of the competitive pack. But that great success was not instantaneous. It took years of planning, engineering, and testing, as well as generous measures of stealth, to make it all come together.

As early as 1953, Deere management under fifth president, Charles Deere Wiman, had decided to replace its two-cylinder tractor engines with four- and six-cylinder engines. Design work on the new tractors took place in an old out-of-the-way grocery store on Falls Avenue in Waterloo, where admittance was only by special pass. Security was extremely tight; knowledge of the tractor designs was restricted to personnel actively involved in the project.

That hush-hush design shop got to be known as the "butcher shop." There the Deere engineers were given their "clean sheet of paper" to advance John Deere tractors to new parameters of performance. The remote butcher shop let them concentrate on the new project away from day-to-day distractions, and it helped them keep the grand project quiet.

The first tractor of the new design was built in 1955 in a steel shed located in a fenced-in area at what is now the Deere & Company Product Engineering Center. The tractor had a V-6 engine with a centered exhaust manifold. It was field tested that fall with a mounted corn picker. Experimental tractors were painted Massey-Ferguson colors and equipped with a wrap-around expanded metal screen to hide their design details from observers with binoculars.

The engineers faced many obstacles, including the fact that to make the existing cross-mounted two-cylinder engines more powerful also meant making the tractor wider. The result would be a tractor too wide to fit between two rows of corn on a row-crop design. That row width had started at about 42 inches (107 cm), the width a draft horse pulling a cultivator needed to pass between two corn rows. Later, when no longer saddled by the physical limits of the horse, new cultural practices worked to narrow that row spacing, first to 40 inches (102 cm), then 38 inches (97 cm), and even 36 inches (91 cm), changes that made it even more imperative not to widen the new, more powerful line of tractors.

The experimental V-type engines first built for the new line had a 45-degree design to keep them as narrow as possible. That engine configuration was later abandoned because it still added too much width to the tractors and too much heat on the operator's legs. An attempt to keep the engines narrow by placing the exhaust manifold in the center was dropped when excess heat buildup there caused problems, too.

John Deere
TEN
TEN

Agricultural
CRAWLER

Tougher, livelier, more versatile—New Generation successor to America's favorite 3-4 plow track-type tractor

JOHN DEERE
WORLD-WIDE

A brochure for the Model 1010 Crawler.

Above: *New track-type tractors from the Dubuque factory were also part of John Deere's New Generation of Power tractors in the 1960s. This 1964 1010 Crawler has the five-roller track option. They were equipped with four-speed sliding-gear transmissions. The 1010 models were available with four-cylinder gasoline or diesel engines of about 30 drawbar hp. Randy Griffin of Letts, Iowa, rebuilt this 1010 agricultural crawler. It mounts a single-shank ripper in its three-point hitch.*

Left: *1010 Crawler steering clutches and instruments.*

THE DREYFUSS TOUCH AGAIN

Henry Dreyfuss's famed industrial design team, whom Deere had relied on for styling and industrial design help since 1937, worked closely with the Deere engineers on the New Generation design and styling. On this project, the Dreyfuss design team got to do something more for the operator of the new tractors: They got to work on designs that would "interface" the operator with the machine. The designers brought in Dr. Janet G. Travell, noted orthopedic physician and back specialist, to help design seats for the new machines. The result of that work provided an operator's seat that could be adjusted to fit people of different sizes. An inclined track mounting for the new posture seat allowed it to be quickly adjusted to operator size and reach. The seat could also be slid all the way up and back to allow the driver to stand periodically to relieve back strain.

There were many surprises inside of the sleek new tractors, too. The new features there led the industry for years. They had been carefully worked out by John Deere planners and engineers in one of the best-kept-industrial-secret product development projects of all time.

The key designers had been given blank sheets of paper to begin their design work in the clandestine butcher shop. But those engineers, each with the responsibility for creating new designs in engines, transmissions, chassis and its control, hydraulics, and hitch arrangements, had definite parameters set out for them on many well-filled-out pieces of paper drawn up by top management, marketing, and manufacturing. They were to accommodate existing John Deere implements, make implement attaching easier, increase horsepower and fuel efficiency, improve operator comfort and convenience, and create improved hydraulic systems for better implement handling and control.

In very early prototype designs some existing two-cylinder-type tractor frames and components were used to create configurations that looked like crossbred models of the 40 and 60 machines. By 1954, prototypes were sporting front fuel tanks, radiator grills on the side, inclined steering gear, and even a seat mounted on an inclined rail. With every prototype there was some progress made. The opening of the new John Deere Waterloo Product Engineering Center in 1956 accelerated engineering

tests. The new engines, now emerging as inline four- and six-cylinder diesel-, gas-, and propane-fueled mills, could go on the dynamometers for testing and re-testing.

Transmissions and engines got their workout on the test track together with the chassis; later prototypes ground their way round and round the track, night and day in all kinds of weather. After thousands of hours of use on the test track, components were torn down, checked for wear, adjusted or modified as needed, and then put back on the test track.

Tractors were cold-tested in the cold room at minus 30 degrees Fahrenheit (-34.4°C) for any cold-prone problems like winter starting. They were tilted in all directions on a tilt table to test for stability and to tell whether slopes effected operations of their fluid-filled components.

Then came the real test: operation in the field under actual-use conditions. Some of the tractors were tested in fields adjoining the test center, others were shipped off to test sites in Texas, Arkansas, and Utah for some more real field work.

John Deere engineers have estimated that by the time the new series was brought out, it had the equivalent testing of ten years of use on the average farm.

DEERE'S GAMBLE PAYS OFF

The years following the introduction of the new tractor line proved the wisdom of Deere's calculated gamble. The company had invested heavily in the New Generation tractors—a product line that was assembled from 95 percent new parts. It took a five-month factory shutdown to complete the changeover from producing the old models to making the new series.

Between introduction in 1960 and the close of the model run in 1963, Deere sold 45,000 3010 tractors, and 57,000 of the larger 4010 tractors.

Farmer acceptance of the new models was outstanding, and the John Deere share of the U.S. tractor market shot up from 23 percent in 1959 to 34 percent in 1964, as the New Generation tractors grew in popularity and sales. By 1963, with the impetus provided by record sales of the New Generation tractor series, John Deere had outpaced rival IHC to become the number one farm and light industrial equipment manufacturer in the United States.

The single-row, row-crop 1010 RS straddled its one row. This 1965 model 1010 was restored by collector Lewis Schleter of Princeton, Indiana. The four-cylinder gas or diesel-equipped 1010 tractors produced about 30 drawbar hp and were considered two-plow tractors. They had a five-speed sliding gear transmission.

Above: *The smallest New Generation tractor was the Dubuque-built Model 1010, which was announced in this 1960 brochure.*

Right: *A compact tractor, compared with the better-known Row-Crop Utility, the 1010 RS had its engine and drive train offset to the left for better single-row vision by the operator. John Deere made five styles of the 1010: the crawler, single row-crop, row-crop utility, row-crop tricycle, and utility. The 1010 was produced from 1960 to 1965.*

A GENERATION OF TRACTORS

In the forty years since the New Generation tractors debuted, John Deere has built on its New Generation lead, introducing a 5010 standard tractor in 1962 that produced more than 100 hp from its two drive wheels—an industry first.

The 4020 came out in 1964 with more power and features than the popular 4010 it replaced. The 4020 diesel produced 91.7 PTO hp and harnessed all of its new "horses" through a new Power Shift transmission, which provided under-load clutchless shifting while underway, through eight gears forward and four in reverse. The 3020 models, also introduced in 1964, produced 65.28 PTO hp. The 3020, too, had the optional Power Shift available (both the 3020 and the 4020 also offered the older Syncro-Range transmission as standard). Both models came with a new hydraulic-power differential lock that directed power equally to both drive wheels when the lock was engaged. More than 177,000 of the 4020s were made from 1964 through 1972, making it the most widely sold single model John Deere of its era. About 86,000 3020 models were sold in that eight-year period.

The 3020 and 4020, built in Waterloo, were joined in 1965 by other tractors in its "family" from Dubuque, including the 1020 and 2020 in low-utility, row-crop utility, or high-utility configurations. The 1020 was a three-cylinder design; the 2020 had four cylinders. The 2020 was available with orchard shielding. Both were available as diesels or gas tractors and were tested at 38.92 and 54.09 PTO hp, respectively.

The 2510 row-crop model replaced the 2010 in 1966. Like its big brothers, it was available with either a Syncro-Range or Power Shift transmission. Its diesel version tested out at 54.96 PTO hp on the Nebraska dynamometer tests. Beginning around 1966, John Deere's specifications indicate only PTO hp, rather than drawbar and PTO hp.

The distinction between row-crop and standard-tread tractors began to fade in the mid-1960s as more owners opted for wide-spaced row-crop front axles rather than the two-wheel narrow-spaced tricycle front that first dominated the row-crop genre. Rear-mounted cultivators hastened that trend to wide-fronts. Chemical weed control materials were reducing the need for close row-crop cultivation.

A more powerful 5020 diesel standard-tread tractor in 1966 bumped the horsepower of the 5010 by 20, testing at 133.25 PTO hp. In 1967, a 5020 Row-Crop version with adjustable wide row-crop front end and 18.4x38-inch (47x97-cm) rear tires was offered by John Deere. With it a farmer could speedily cultivate 30-inch (76-cm) narrow rows with a twelve-row rear-mounted cultivator.

Power Shift transmissions were available for on-the-go shifting in the improved 3020 and 4020 models introduced in 1964. This 1964 gasoline 3020 has been recently restored by Bruce Halverson of Huxley, Iowa. It has the adjustable wide front end for use in row crops.

Above: *Classic styling first seen in 1960 on the New Generation tractors stayed with the upgraded 3020 and 4020 of 1964. The tractor models remained in production until 1972 and were replaced by the Generation II models in 1973.*

Right: *More powerful engines put out 64 PTO hp on the 3020 gasoline-fueled models, nearly 10 hp more than the 3010 it replaced. A foot-pedal-operated hydraulic power differential lock helped the 3020 and 4020 pull more in slick conditions by equalizing power to the drive wheels. This 1964 3020 is owned by Bruce Halverson.*

The John Deere Model 4020 is considered the firm's all-time classic tractor. Derived from the 4010 introduced in 1960, the famous 4020 replaced it in 1964. This original-condition 1965 gasoline 4020 is still helping its farmer-collector owner, Tom Manning of Dallas Center, Iowa, produce corn and soybeans.

Top: *More horsepower and new features added to the appeal of the new Models 3020 and 4020 that Deere brought out in 1964 to replace the 3010 and 4010 tractors.*

Bottom: *Shifting through eight forward speeds without clutching was the forte of the optional Power Shift transmission available on the 3020 and 4020 tractors. The less-expensive Synchro-Range transmission was still available.*

Above: *Deep fall chisel-plowing of heavy prairie soils began to replace moldboard plowing over parts of the Corn Belt in the late 1960s. This 5020 diesel, with an add-on cab, is chiseling disked corn stalks in Woodford County, Illinois, in an early trial of "conservation tillage."*

Left: *This highly stylized leaping deer was registered as the company's primary trademark in 1969. Memorabilia collectors call it the two-legged leaping deer trademark. (Deere & Company archives)*

THE 820, 1520, 2520, AND 4000

The 820, a three-cylinder diesel utility model introduced in 1968, was at the low end of power sizes provided by Deere in the New Generation series. It was a product of Deere's growing foreign operations and was made in Germany by the John Deere Mannheim Works, using Deere's new worldwide design. At an estimated 31 PTO hp, it was the smallest of the John Deere line.

The 1520 model of 1968 offered the smaller-tractor buyer a 46.52-PTO-hp John Deere machine to fit between the 1020 and 2020 tractors.

Engine improvements from the Waterloo plant in 1969 again changed the row-crop tractor offerings from John Deere. Improved piston and ring design, changes to the cylinder block and liner, a new dry-type air cleaner, and a 12-volt electrical system with alternator, gave new specifications of 61.29 PTO horsepower to the new 2520 tractor that replaced the 2510.

The Model 4000, produced from 1969 to 1972, was designed as a no-frills tractor for the farmer who wanted a move up in power from the 3020 at a cost less than the 4020. It had the same engine as the 4020 with a tested PTO output of 96.89 hp. It was designed to pull a four-bottom plow at a faster speed than a five-plow tractor, matching the bigger tractor's work output.

THE TURBOCHARGED 4520 AND THE SUPER 4020

The 4520 was the first of John Deere's turbocharged "Turbo-Built" tractors manufactured. Its factory-installed turbocharger packed additional air into its diesel engine so more fuel could be burned to produce more power per stroke. Deere engineers gave the engine more lubricating capacity, a bigger radiator and fan, an improved block for increased coolant flow for better cooling of the more powerful engine, and a bigger air cleaner for easier "breathing." That Turbo-Built design also included stronger drive train components to handle the extra power produced by the puffed-up engine. The 4520, manufactured from 1969 to 1970, tested 122.36 PTO hp at Nebraska in 1969.

More "heavy breathing" was designed into the 4320, or the so-called super 4020, introduced in 1970 and sold in 1971 and 1972. It produced about 21 percent more power than the naturally aspirated 4020, weighed nearly 700 pounds (318 kg) more, and sported wider 20.8x34-inch (53x86-cm) rear tires to better transfer its greater power to the ground. The 4320 rated 116.55 PTO hp compared with 91.17 from the 4020 in its original Nebraska tests.

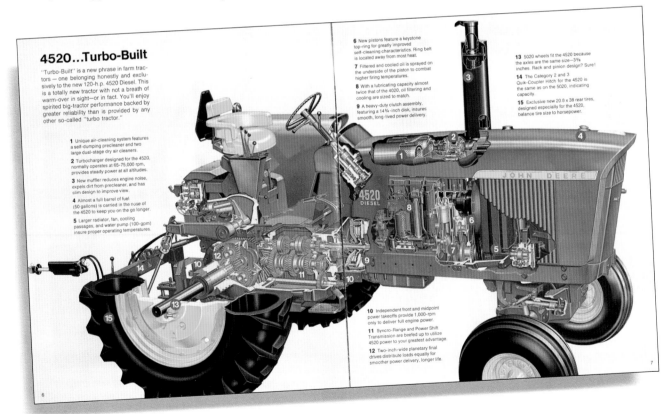

The first turbocharged farm tractor was the 122.36-hp John Deere Model 4520. Manufactured in 1969 and 1970, the 4520 was "Turbo-Built" with beefed-up components to handle the extra horsepower.

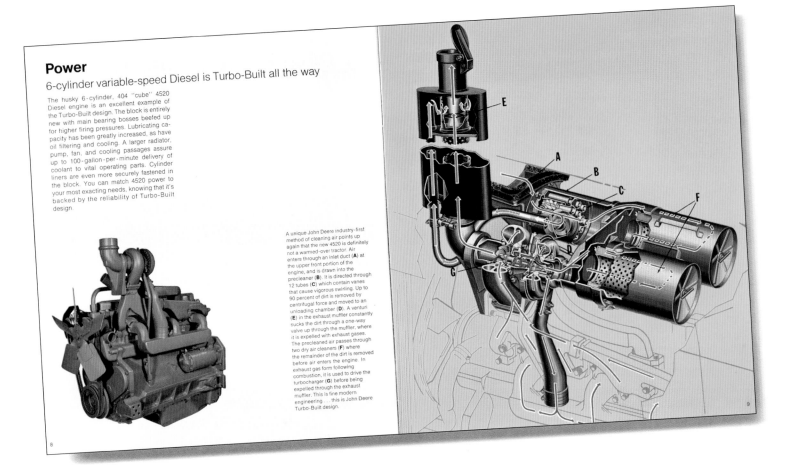

Power

6-cylinder variable-speed Diesel is Turbo-Built all the way

The husky 6-cylinder, 404 "cube" 4520 Diesel engine is an excellent example of the Turbo-Built design. The block is entirely new with main bearing bosses beefed up for higher firing pressures. Lubricating capacity has been greatly increased, as have oil filtering and cooling. A larger radiator, pump, fan, and cooling passages assure up to 100-gallon-per-minute delivery of coolant to vital operating parts. Cylinder liners are even more securely fastened in the block. You can match 4520 power to your most exacting needs, knowing that it's backed by the reliability of Turbo-Built design.

A unique John Deere industry-first method of cleaning air points up again that the new 4520 is definitely not a warmed-over tractor. Air enters through an inlet duct (**A**) at the upper front portion of the engine, and is drawn into the precleaner (**B**). It is directed through 12 tubes (**C**) which contain vanes that cause vigorous swirling. Up to 90 percent of dirt is removed by centrifugal force and moved to an unloading chamber (**D**). A venturi (**E**) in the exhaust muffler constantly sucks the dirt through a one-way valve up through the muffler, where it is expelled with exhaust gases. The precleaned air passes through two dry air cleaners (**F**) where the remainder of the dirt is removed before air enters the engine. In exhaust gas form following combustion, it is used to drive the turbocharger (**G**) before being expelled through the exhaust muffler. This is fine modern engineering . . . this is John Deere Turbo-Built design.

John Deere explained its 4520 turbocharger in product literature.

TURBOCHARGED-INTERCOOLED 4620

In another industry first, John Deere brought out intercooling on the turbocharged Model 4620, introduced in 1971. John Deere engineers used an intake manifold intercooler on the 4620 to cool turbocharged intake air before it was pushed into the cylinders. Since compressing intake air by turbocharging heats the air and makes it less dense, cooling that heated compressed air before combustion allows more air density, providing the engine more oxygen per power stroke for added power and efficiency.

To accommodate increased horsepower, the 4620 tractor was Turbo-Built with strengthened final drives, axles, and frame and equipped with a 1,000-rpm PTO.

The 4620 was rated at 135.62 PTO hp.

THE 7020, 7520, AND 6030

Row-crop capabilities in a four-wheel-drive tractor was first offered by John Deere with the 1970 introduction of its 146.17-PTO-hp 7020 model. Its articulated steering design placed the operator's cab on the front frame be-

hind the engine. A wide variety of wheel spacings allowed it to be fitted to a range of row widths, and 18.4-inch (47-cm) tires could be dualed on all four wheels to fit between narrow rows.

A 175.82-PTO-hp version of the row-crop-capable, four-wheel-drive articulated-steering tractor, the 7520, was made from 1972 to 1975. Its power came from a new six-cylinder turbocharged-intercooled diesel engine with a 531-cubic-inch (8,701-cc) displacement. The 7520 came with a Roll-Gard cab standard. Heating and air conditioning were optional. Like its smaller sibling, the 7020, it could be equipped and adjusted to negotiate narrow-row crops. Its four driving axles could carry dual tires for the extra traction needed in soft or loose soil conditions.

The largest two-wheel-drive tractor in the New Generation line was the burly 6030 model built from 1972 to 1977. It was powered by the same turbocharged-intercooled six-cylinder diesel used in the four-wheel-drive 7520. It was built in both standard-tread and row-crop configurations. Dual tires could be added to give the tractor the grip it needed to harness its 175.99 PTO hp.

The 6030 was the evolutionary extension of the big 5010 John Deere whose horsepower of 121.2 PTO topped the New Generation tractors at its introduction in 1963. Nearly ten years later, through advancements in engine design and technology, the 6030 packed nearly 55 more horsepower than the original 5010 design. And the horsepower race was not over.

By 1972, John Deere tractors were well beyond the 100-horsepower level, had even passed 150, and were climbing toward the 200 level. That year, the New Generation of Power machines introduced in the Cotton Bowl fanfare of 1960 were replaced with Generation II models. Just three years later, the 8630 model of 1975 passed the 200-horsepower mark by quite a bit, hitting 225.59 PTO hp. By the early 1980s John Deere had an "Iron Horse" in its stable showing more than 300 PTO hp: The 1982 Model 8850 tested at 303.99 PTO hp.

A New Century of Power

As horsepower levels and farm implement production grew, so did the company. Who knows what power levels will be seen in the future?

Born in the prairies and nurtured by the emergence of the Corn Belt from those vast grass oceans, Deere & Company continues its growth from humble prairie roots into a world-class company serving agriculture around the globe.

Deere & Company profits passed $1 billion for the first time in 1998, reaching record levels for the fifth year in a row, as Hans W. Becherer, Chairman and Chief Executive Officer, reported at the company's 1999 annual meeting.

As the twenty-first century begins, Deere & Company continues that growth despite slumping prices for grain and livestock in the heart of its domestic market area. With agricultural equipment counting for only about half of total revenues, the company depends less today on that sector of the economy and sees a bright future ahead.

After more than 164 years, Deere & Company, started by one man with a better idea for a prairie plow, continues to provide constantly improving John Deere farm equipment for farmers who produce the food and fiber needed to make the world a better place to live. And aficionados of the green-and-yellow machines continue to show their appreciation with their acquisition, loving restoration, and preservation of vintage John Deere tractors.

This new John Deere trademark was introduced in mid-2000. For the first time, the stylized deer in the trademark is leaping confidently upward instead of landing on outstretched front legs as in previous versions. Deere & Company says the new brand mark moves John Deere forward into the new millennium with confidence and power.

Bibliography

Arnold, Dave. *Vintage John Deere*. Stillwater, Minn.: Voyageur Press, 1995.

Atherton, Lewis E. *The Frontier Merchant in Mid-America*. Columbia: University of Missouri, 1971.

Bogue, Allan G. *From Prairie to Corn Belt: Farming on the Illinois and Iowa Prairies in the Nineteenth Century*. Ames: Iowa State University Press, 1994.

Bradford, William. *Of Plymouth Plantation, 1620–1647*. Edited by Samuel Eliot Morison. New York: Alfred A. Knopf, 1996.

Broehl, Wayne G., Jr. *John Deere's Company: A History of Deere & Company and Its Times*. New York: Doubleday & Company, 1984.

Brown, Dee; with Martin F. Schmitt. *Trail Driving Days*. New York: Ballantine Books, 1974.

Brown, Theo. *Deere & Company's Early Tractor Development*. Grundy Center, Iowa: Two-Cylinder Club, with permission from Deere & Company, 1997.

Catton, Bruce. *The Civil War*. New York: American Heritage Publishing Co., Inc., 1982.

Clark, Neil M. *John Deere: He Gave to the World the Steel Plow*. Moline, Ill.: privately printed, 1937.

Clark, Thomas D. *Pills, Petticoats and Plows: The Southern Country Store*. Indianapolis: The Bobbs-Merrill Company, 1944.

Covich, Edith Sklovsky. *MAX*. Chicago: Stuart Brent, 1974.

Deere & Company. *John Deere Tractors: 1918–1994*. St. Joseph, Mich.: American Society of Agricultural Engineers, 1994.

Dreyfuss, Henry. *Designing for People*. New York: Grossman, 1967.

Erb, David and Eldon Brumbaugh. *Full Steam Ahead: J. I. Case Tractors & Equipment 1842–1955*. St. Joseph, Mich.: American Society of Agricultural Engineers, 1993.

Flinchum, Russell. *Henry Dreyfuss Industrial Designer: The Man in the Brown Suit*. New York: Rizzoli International, 1997.

Furrow, The, editors. *The Furrow-Bicentennial Issue*. Moline, Ill.: Deere & Company, 1975.

———. *The Furrow—Special 100th Anniversary*. Moline, Ill.: Deere & Company, 1995.

Gay, Larry. *Farm Tractors: 1975–1995*. St. Joseph, Mich.: American Society of Agricultural Engineers, 1995.

Gray, R. B. *The Agricultural Tractor: 1855–1950*. St. Joseph, Mich.: American Society of Agricultural Engineers, 1954.

Huber, Donald S. and Ralph C. Hughes. *How Johnny Popper Replaced the Horse: A History of John Deere Two-Cylinder Tractors*. Moline, Ill.: Deere & Company, 1988.

Hunter, Louis C. *Steamboats on the Western Rivers: An Economic and Technological History*. New York: Dover Publications, 1993.

John Deere engineers and editors. *The Operation, Care and Repair of Farm Machinery*, 21st ed. Moline, Ill.: Deere & Company, n.d.

John Garnett H & Co. *Catalogue of Agricultural and Horticultural Implements and Machines*. St. Louis: 1858.

Johnson, Charles Beneulyn, M.D. *Illinois in the Fifties; or, A Decade of Development, 1851–1860*. Champaign, Ill.: Flanigan-Pearson, 1918.

Johnson, Paul C. *Farm Animals in the Making of America*. Decorah, Iowa: Institute for Agricultural Biodiversity, 1993.

———. *Farm Inventions in the Making of America*. Decorah, Iowa: Institute for Agricultural Biodiversity, 1993.

———. *Farm Power in the Making of America*. Decorah, Iowa: Institute for Agricultural Biodiversity, 1993.

Kendall, Edward C. *John Deere's Steel Plow*. Bulletin 218. Washington, D.C.: United States National Museum, Smithsonian Institution, 1959.

Larson, Lester. *Farm Tractors, 1950–1975*. St. Joseph, Mich.: American Society of Agricultural Engineers, 1981.

Macmillan, Don. *The Big Book of John Deere Tractors: The Complete Model-By-Model Encyclopedia, plus Classic Toys, Brochures, and Collectibles*. Stillwater, Minn.:

Voyageur Press, 1999.

Macmillan, Don, and Roy Harrington. *John Deere Tractors and Equipment, Volume II, 1960–1990.* St. Joseph, Mich.: American Society of Agricultural Engineers, 1991.

Macmillan, Don, and Russell Jones. *John Deere Tractors and Equipment: 1837–1959.* St. Joseph, Mich.: American Society of Agricultural Engineers, 1988.

Peterson, Chester, Jr., and Rod Beemer. *John Deere New Generation Tractors.* Osceola, Wisc.: Motorbooks International, 1998.

Pooley, William Vipond. *The Settlement of Illinois from 1830 to 1850.* Madison: University of Wisconsin, 1908.

Prairie Farmer editors. "Farm Power From Muscle to Motor, Revolution in Rubber, Plows that Made the Prairies, Sowing and Growing, The Better the Fuel. . . ." *Prairie Farmer,* Jan. 11, 1941.

Pripps, Robert N. *Vintage Ford Tractors.* Stillwater, Minn.: Voyageur Press, 1997.

Sanders, Ralph W. *Vintage Farm Tractors.* Stillwater, Minn.: Voyageur Press, 1996.

———. *Vintage International Harvester Tractors.* Stillwater, Minn.: Voyageur Press, 1997.

U.S. Department of Agriculture. *Climate and Man: The Yearbook of Agriculture, 1941.* Washington, D.C.: U.S. Government Printing Office, 1941.

———. *Power to Produce: The Yearbook of Agriculture, 1960.* Washington, D.C.: U.S. Government Printing Office, 1960.

Van Syoc, Wendell M. *Life with Deere & Company: 1948–1984.* Cedar Falls, Iowa: unpublished manuscript, 1997.

Wendel, C. H. *Encyclopedia of American Farm Tractors.* Osceola, Wisc.: Motorbooks International, 1992.

———. *150 Years of International Harvester.* Osceola, Wisc.: Motorbooks International, 1993.

Wilkinson, H. E. *Memories of an Iowa Farm Boy.* Ames: Iowa State University Press, 1994.

Wm. Koenig & Co. *Reduced Price List for 1875 of the Jno. Deere Moline Plows.* St. Louis: Wm. Koenig & Co., 1874.

Index

About the Author

Ralph W. Sanders was born and raised on a prairie farm near Stonington, Illinois, where his great-great grandfather, J. Nicholas Sanders, settled with his family in 1837. That was the same spring John Deere got his new plow to self-scour in the northern part of the state, about 160 miles (259 km) north-northwest of Stonington, at Grand Detour. Except for that coincidence in dates, John Deere and Nicholas Sanders probably had little else in common except they were both Yankees of about the same age who had cast their lot in the West. Both were soon to learn a great deal from the prairies. Ralph's great-great grandfather moved to Illinois from near the small town of Voluntown in eastern Connecticut. Deere was from the Rutland area in west-central Vermont and moved to Illinois from the village of Hancock.

The last team of horses left the fifth-generation Sanders farm when Ralph was only five, so he grew up driving tractors—beginning almost before he could reach the clutch. Ralph also missed out on shocking wheat and oats and pitching bundles into a threshing machine. He did, however, get to be the "header-tender" on a 1929 pull-type Holt Model 36 combine his father, John, operated on the family farm until 1955.

As a boy and young man helping on the farm, Ralph learned some things about the prairie, too. One was to always keep your plow polished so it would scour the next time you plowed. Axle grease smeared on the moldboard and plowshare helped it maintain its "dirt-polish" until it went in the ground again a season later. Short-term protection came from a quick treatment with used crankcase oil. Let the polished plow rust, and it was a hassle to get it to scour again. That struggle must have been akin to what the early prairie farmers experienced on prairie soils with their cast-iron plows.

Another lesson learned was that spring thunderstorms moved across the prairie fields faster than could the farm tractors he drove as a boy. He and his brothers, Jack and Jim, usually got drenched when they tried to outrun the showers on the old tractors as they raced from the fields to the tractor shed at a roaring five miles per hour.

With many hundred hours invested on the tractor seats of his youth, Ralph continued his love of tractors as the years passed, and, forty years later, he got to chronicle their return in importance as antiques and classic collectibles.

After a stint in the U.S. Army in Germany from 1954 to 1956, Ralph returned to college and, in 1958, earned his bachelors degree in journalism at the University of Illinois at Urbana.

Copyright © 2000 by Rich Sanders

He worked as a broadcast journalist at radio stations WCRA in Effingham, Illinois, in 1958–1959 and at WDZ in Decatur, Illinois, in 1959–1961. He then became a reporter for the Decatur *Herald & Review.* From 1964 to 1968, he was Illinois field editor for *Prairie Farmer* magazine. He joined *Successful Farming* magazine in Des Moines, Iowa, as an associate editor in 1968. In 1974, he followed his long-term passion for photography and became a full-time self-employed freelance photographer in Des Moines.

Agricultural, advertising, and industrial photography for a long list of clients kept him challenged for the next twenty-two years. Assignments for Deere & Company's advertising department were an important part of his work between 1974 and 1981. During those years, Ralph had the opportunity to photograph John Deere farm and industrial equipment in a wide range of locations across the United States and into Canada. Those experiences deepened his appreciation of the company and its line of productive John Deere machines.

Ralph, and his wife of more than forty years, Joanne, have seven grown children and eleven grandchildren. They have lived in West Des Moines, Iowa, for thirty-two years.

Ralph and Joanne travel as many as 20,000 miles (32,000 km) each year photographing antique tractors and meeting the nicest people in the world: those who cherish and collect antique farm tractors.

Ralph has photographed antique tractors for all twelve annual issues of the *Classic Farm Tractors* calendar, distributed since 1990 by DuPont Agricultural Chemicals. He also photographs and writes the *Historic Farm Tractors* and *Classic John Deere Tractors* calendars, published annually by Voyageur Press.

In addition, Ralph is the author and photographer of the Voyageur Press books *Vintage Farm Tractors* (1996) and *Vintage International Harvester Tractors* (1997). This is Ralph's third book.